Starving My Past Feeding My Future

By: Tinker Jeffries

Before I began to write this book. I wrote, "My New Book Sold a Million Copies" everywhere on all mirrors in my apartment, on sticky notes on the walls, on the computer, and on the visor in my car to remind me that this book will sell plenty. This book is the therapy to give me the realization of myself and to allow others to get to know the author's deepest black heart.

Put God first in everything. I'm a firm believer in this. Therefore, I want to thank God for giving me the amazing gift of putting words together. This time in this third book, he gave me the power to write without stumbling or freezing my brain. Each day the words flowed gradually.

Second, I want to thank my readers and believers who have stuck with me and are still with me since 2008 when I began to write erotic blogs. You all are absolutely awesome. There's this one reader I will never forget. She said, "Your story gave me life throughout college." Now she's married and is an RN in a hospital in Atlanta. There's so many more who grew with me.

I can't do a dedication without saying thank you to my parents and love ones. So special thanks to my Mother and Step-Father (Mr. Darrell) for laying out a blueprint to life. My Father. My father is the example of a man that had plentiful of women. He Found God, changed his life entirely then got married. If he can be a loyal man, I believe anyone can. My dad was literally there for the streets. Thank you to my brother Devon. I honestly can write a whole page on him. My younger brother Devon is actually my neighbor. The access of having him downstairs is incredible. He's my personal life coach and will hold me accountable for my wrongdoings. He gets me clearly when I'm glaring through a foggy lens. Also, his work ethic with spending long hours in school to become a chaplain; motivated me that I can reach my goals. Afro Puff is what Devon calls you. Sister Linsey thank you for making my brother this amazing man. Everything I do is for my four children My brother Braylon, Thanks for always being there when I needed you. I hardly speak to my sisters but I hope to build a relationship with both of you. Brother Daequan Hardly. I hope to build a stronger relationship with you as well. I enjoy watching you on television on Saturdays. Baby Cousin Jaiden White, Uncle Dino, Aunt Taunya, and Mama (Grandma) I love you all.

Can't forget my best friends Wade Jones. Our friendship is unbreakable. Love you fool.

Los Boogie. My Dawg until the end. Great Dad and someone I can call whenever advice. Love you.

During writing the book, Rayne Shine was a good friend and my accountable partner. After every chapter was written she would give me the input on the story. Thank you for being there through this long process.

I want to give a big Thanks to Charade Jones for editing my book in the clutch. Charade took my book in then went straight to work. Thank you again.

Music I listened to while writing this book.

UGK, Outcast, FKJ, Masego, Jill Scott, Curren$y, Chevy Wood, D Smoke, J.Cole, Big Sean, Daniel Caesar, Eric Bellinger, and so many others. Tommy Brown (Producer) showed it's possible to reach beyond the stars.

Starving My Past Fccding My Future

001. The End

I was a ladies' man. Dealing with hundreds of women taught me the game. I was lethal or what the social world calls now of days, "toxic" to some people and a blessing to others. I honestly can admit I wasn't always in the right. Understand we all have flaws and God didn't make me or you perfect that's just the beauty of being human. I've done shredded hearts into insignificant pieces; broken trust barrels, and deceived and mislead plenty of women.

On the flip side, I've been dogged by women who I truly provided and cared for. It's amusing when you actually care for somebody and those individuals will treat you the worst. Those individuals that you mistreat will adore you the most. This dating shit is backward. I've been in multiple relationships from lengths of one year, two years, and the longest relationship that lasted for four years. Love is a mothafucka but to me, the trust holds more weight than anything. Fully giving yourself to someone, being honest, and not being selfish; investing your time and money into a relationship can be a full-time job. Yet, a relationship can be the best situation that can happen to someone. Adventures, traveling, conversations, dates, gifts, and intimate and spontaneous sex and building each other to be greater.

There are tons of benefits that come with being connected with someone. And to be truthful your relationship will be such a success if you have God in the middle.

These words are fully about my journey with multiple women I'm not writing this book to expose anyone. To protect myself from getting sued and peoples' characters I'll be using fabricated names. Everything I've learned when it comes to relationships, sex, or just affairs with women will be written in this book. For all the women I hurt in the past, I wish I could call every one of you to apologize for my young behavior. Here we go "Starving My Past Feeding My Future."

Bet sometimes in your life you glanced at someone who wasn't on the television. They were just a stranger you didn't have a clue about and wondered how this person's living situation was. What's was their story? What were their struggles? What were their strengths and weaknesses? I do this all the time. I'm the stranger and this is my story.

Honestly, this is the most difficult shit to write an autobiography of myself, there are many times I would type at least five thousand words then delete the whole story. But fuck it I'm just going to write this story from my point of view simply because it's my story. I'm not famous nor do I have thousands of dollars. I'm just a regular man with a regular job who had hundreds and hundreds of women.

"Why you write sex stories? Are they based on your personal life or are they fictional?" These are the questions my readers always ask me. Well, my imagination is creative but at the same time, my sexual experience helped to give details on the sex scenes in my stories. Once upon a time, you could say I was a man-whore, I had a serious addiction to sex. Each night there was a different woman staying overnight, I couldn't sleep without a dose of some wet pussy to sink in. On the nights, I didn't have anyone available I had an RTCC (Round the Corner Chick), those were chicks who lived within walking distance from home. They would come out any hour of the night. Most of the time they were the mediocre chicks who were down for whatever and whenever.

My past wasn't the greatest in some eyes but it was that same experience that taught me so much about what women like, how their thinking process, how a woman likes to be treated, how to pleasure a woman sexually, mentally, and emotionally and how to love (but the one thing it didn't teach me was how to love spiritually. I learned that later in life as I started to follow God). I'm sharing this to get the old ways out of my system before I say my "I do's," and jump the broom with the woman of my dreams.

I don't regret my hoeish past for the fact that the words I express have my books flying off the internet, married couples and couples, in general, are booking me to strengthen their sex lives. I guess I am a sex therapist without a degree. Females book me for pajama parties and toy parties to sit and tell live sex stories, I entertain groups of women and make pussies wet just from telling erotic tales. All I'm saying is I lived the sexual life to tell my story

…

March 17, 2019

It was Saturday night and I was sitting on the couch beside the woman I proposed to a year prior. The light beamed out of the 50-inch television filling the corners of the dark living room. Before this moment, my fiancée and I had a spectacular day full of smiles, great conversation, and good energy we shared, despite the complication we had dealt with for the past months. No relationship is perfect I don't give a damn how pure we appeared to the outside world. Social media is just a highlight reel being judged by public visuals; inside the house, shit was out of place.

"What's your password to your Instagram?" She asked glaring at me squinting her eyes with suspicion written all over her amber face.

"For what? You mess that up last time you had access to my Instagram." A few months prior, she had access to all social media platforms that I utilized daily. The privilege was taken away when she responded to compliments by women followers in the direct messages. Most of the time when I got a friendly compliment from a woman I would double-tap the comment to show my appreciation. I'm an author with real believers, readers, and fans so for me to ignore them would be rude. Especially if a reader supported me by buying books or merchandise. On the other hand, everyone that followed me on Instagram knew I had a woman that I was deeply in love with so if anyone left disrespectful comments I would just leave the person on read. The day she took things into her own hands to argue with someone through the direct messaging was the day I changed the password. After this day, our relationship took a jump off the highest building in the world.

"I only made one mistake, you made a lot and you're still holding this over my head."

"Well, I'm not giving you my password," I said surly

"Let me see your phone then."

There was not nothing in my phone; I deleted all messages that should not be in the threads before the trip home from Morgantown, West Virginia. I usually drove there and back every Saturday morning for work.

"No, why you want to see my phone?"

The Seinfeld show was on the television; we both turned our attention to the show while we traded awkward energy.

"I can't believe I was going marry a nigga that won't give me his password for Instagram." She gleamed at me with disgust.

"Damn we had a good day. Now we're going end it like this." I said shaking my head. I pulled my iPhone out of my pocket then began to scroll through my Instagram. I felt her eyes drilling a hole through my soul while I continued to be unbothered. Not even a minute with my phone out in the open she swiftly abducted my phone then darted through the dining room into the kitchen to grasp the biggest cutting knife. I did not chase her down I just walked behind her nonchalantly for the fact I knew there was not nothing in my phone to get me caught up.

"Don't you come near me. I will fucking stab you!" She heaved heavily, nose flaring wider than a bull with a knife in shaky hands.

"You can have the phone. You're not going to find nothing."

I was certain. She backed out of the kitchen then went up the steps that went to the second floor. I strolled to the living room with no worries then flopped on the couch to continue watching Seinfeld. 40 minutes later I heard the squeaking bathroom door open. I heard the love of my life moan with pain.

"Oh my God. I miss you!" She said once. "I miss you though." She said again.

I heard footsteps move expeditiously on the wooden floor.

I knew that she came across something but I was not sure what she would've detected. My hands were moistening and my heart was beating off rhythm and what I had done earlier before coming home from West Virginia was probably the karma that ended us for good. At turtle pace, she crept down the wood-cracking stairwell with a 45-mm gun in hand. Tears streamed down her distressful face while her hair went every which way.

"How could you? After all, I've done for you. How could you Darren?"

"What I do?" I wasn't startled not one bit because the safety was on. I was more scared of her with a knife than a gun.

"She misses you already."

"What are you talking about?" I had an idea who the woman was but I still played dumb.

"Darren don't act fucking stupid."

She took another step down.

"Put that gun down."

"She fucking misses you."

Now I was getting nervous; she was furious. She lifted the gun breathing heavily with the finger on the trigger then

"POW"

12 Hours Earlier.

It was a sunny Saturday afternoon after delivering the medicine in Morgantown West Virginia for work, I detoured my way to Cal-U college to visit Cassidy. How I met Cassidy was on Instagram via messaging. She heart-eyed a video in my story, I responded with a simple "You're going to have an amazing day." which turned into a full-blown conversation. She mentioned that her week was a complete disaster and my manifestation for her was the best words she heard that week.

My life was in a downswing at home as well. First, my relationship was falling apart, my fiancée wrote a long letter stating that it was best for us to separate after four years, and then on top of that she withdrew sex for approximately two months prior. Her reason for taking away intercourse was because she wanted to wait until we got married. Granted this was after we had our child but I was okay with her decision. I was all for waiting until the day we tie the knot. It's just happened abruptly. She abandoned sex cold turkey followed after a five-minute conversation. As the days passed I became addicted to porn and on social media more than usual. I was on the far side of being sexually frustrated. I honestly thought we both were frustrated, we argued regarding the smallest shit. It was like we were growing apart by the hour. There were days we did not even speak. We would just walk past one another as if we were blind.

So, when I was at Cassidy's place the connection was evident. We were both tender and facing some life predicaments. She was a young petite redbone, appealing to the eyes with long black curly natural hair that stopped in the middle of the back. Cassidy was exceedingly affectionate; our welcome hug lasted for a good minute, which ended with a kiss on her forehead. She was full of energy, despite whatever was happening in her life. She hid it behind her smile and outgoing personality. Whereas at my home it seemed so dark, cloudy, and doleful. At this moment with Cassidy, the vibe was like a sunny day in spring.

Cassidy shared an apartment with a roommate who left for spring break. The unit was separated into two places. Each section of the apartment had an office, a bedroom, and a bathroom with a huge mirror behind a sink. Between the private rooms, there was a kitchen and a furnished living room. They were actually living comfortably for two young college students. Her office was filled with photos on the wall of friends and family, stuffed animals in the corner of the room, and a bookshelf full of books and few decorations. Her bedroom was plain; there was a twin-size bed and a 32' inch television playing the MTV show Ridiculousness. I can't explain the situation she was dealing with but it was a strenuous time she dealt with annually. We laughed at the show momentary as we watched TV but for the most part we shared conversation. When she removed her school pride sweatpants then laid in the bed dressed in panties, colorful high socks, and a spaghetti strap crop top, I positioned myself beside her thin body and held her as if she was my woman. At this time, the woman at home did not exist. I brought Cassidy comforted and most importantly, I listened. By bringing those needed qualities, the bond was deeper on her end. On my end, I fed her the needs to make her fall for me so cavernously she was open for me to plant soft kisses on her neck, collar and the nape of her neck. Her body shifted from each kiss as her moans poured while she breathed heavily. I was beyond aroused. It had been almost two months since I felt the warmth of a woman. When she pushed her ass against my shaft it grew hard to its full potential; throbbing damn near begging for the pussy.

"I want you," I whispered in her ear.

She snuggled her booty against me and that was all the reply I needed. I usually would caress a woman's entire body to get her aroused to the breaking point. I would edge her to get the pussy extremely wet. A woman has a complete body to play with. She has more than just a pussy and two nipples. If a man played around those areas; like biting the inner thighs, kissing on the pelvis, deep passionate massages, kissing and licking from her neck to the toes or briefly licking or sucking on the hot spots; you would spike her sexual excitement. When it came time to swaddle the lip around her clit so you can glide your tongue across or plug your pipe inside her vagina she would be set to climax as soon as you stimulated her.

This was a different scenario; I was past horny and my selfish need for sex had me disregard the foreplay and forget I was hanging on by a thread in my relationship. I adjusted myself between her frail legs, slid the panties to the side, leaned my face amidst her thighs then I bundled my lips around her clitoris with a mouth full of saliva. I slithered my tongue slowly against her love button. Her body twitched as if I switched on a power generator, not more than one lap across her clit I noticed her spot by the response her body signaled. Cassidy's stomach sank in alternating motion (in and out). She had no control of her hands, they were gripping sheets, pillows, scratching walls, and unsystematically waving all over the bed while her moans filled the room with pleasure. My tongue slid back and forth across the clit at a mild pace attacking for her to climax over my lips. Not even five minutes of devouring her passion fruit her body went rigid and like an air mattress, her skin deflated into her bones as her legs quivered, between curse words and gasp of moans. Minutes after she regained her composure and she kindly returned the favor. She placed herself between my thighs, as I lie flat on the twin bed with just a t-shirt and socks on. As she grasped hold of my 23 centimeters' curved midnight manhood, I felt her lengthy curly hair brush against my stomach before her mouth took me in fully. In combination, her pretty face yoyo'd simultaneously as her hands stroked and drool cascaded down to the root. It had been a while since someone touched me in such a way therefore, my dick was utterly sensitive.

"Suck that shit," I uttered seldom probably biting my lip as I gained possession of her hair in a balled fist as her face continued to suck all my issues away. Erotic noises of slurping in unison with soft moans had me on the verge of spouting white juices. I had other plans than cumming from a blowjob. I was yearning for pussy. In the midst of getting slobbed down, I interrupted by pulling her hair back. She glared up with a slight smile.

"Sit on it," I demanded glimpsing down at her messy face.

Cassidy hovered over my soaking black manhood coated with her mucus. She held the stem as she gradually drifted down. She was more breathtaking with each inch she absorbed. Her love box was ultra-tight gripping, warm, and supremely wet. My toes curled in the moment she seesawed upward and downward, alternately on my pole. To be honest a lengthy sex session of more than five or ten minutes to an hour was out of the question. First, my goal was to make her cum. And if I was to cum before her I would eat her until she did so.

One fact I teach when I counsel couples is to not be selfish. Sex is an unselfish deed. When both are core to satisfy one another, that's when intercourse is glorious. So even if she doesn't climax off the dick I had to come up with other ways to make her overflow. At the end of it all, she melted on my shaft as she rode. Not even a second after I came I felt a scramble of remorse. In this situation, I was not thinking with my head but just my dick head. When the lustful feeling of the chase of pussy diminished, reality struck especially when the shit hit the fan later that night.

Twenty minutes of playing the field could get you kicked out of the game permanently. Due to the fact, I had a guilty conscience I treated my ex to dinner just to sow the guilt I was concealing. Dinner or an incredible time did not stop the universe to allow my inconsiderate infidelity act to remain in the dark.

12 Hours Before

"Pow" she never shot the gun but shot me by leaving our four-year relationship. This was when life took a dramatic change. I never thought in a million years I would be at stage one again in the single category.

002. Depression

Literally a month after the disturbing break-up, we broke the lease and I moved into a new two-bedroom apartment on the north side of Pittsburgh, Shit was just different. I was not used to living without a family, daily routine, or being alone for the majority of the day; and while being lonely remorseful thoughts flooded my mind. One thing people are attached to is our memories of the good times they spent with their significant other. The beginning of the relationship, the moment you two laughed so hard both of your stomachs were hurting and tears of laughter streamed down. The vacation, the day you were at your lowest and they were there when you desperately needed them by your side and the breathtaking sex. Thoughts of the cheating crossed your mind and when she caught me replayed it a thousand times. For me, those thoughts brought depression into the story. For the first month, my daily routine was getting up at 5:30 am Drinking my Herbalife shake and tea which supported me to lose 45 pounds, get dressed then be at the warehouse to load my cargo van at 6:30 am. I finished deliveries an hour after the afternoon every day. I would run four to five miles depending on the weather or get it in at the gym for an hour or two. I would come home and cook and eat dinner, take a shower then the remainder of the day I would sit on the edge of the bed pondering or scrolling through social media where everyone seems to be happy.

Snapping out of depression was not mindless at this point I knew I had to get out of the house and find happiness somewhere. The streets were calling me. It was time for me to date again because being in the house for 30 to 40 days I began to rot mentally. I attempted to reach out to my old hoes who would slide in my direct messages from time to time. Two of them had boyfriends out of the blue, one played and never came over, another left me on read. My lifetime side bitch got into a serious relationship. There was a time I could say, "come through." And she would've paused whatever she was doing to come get this dick. It seemed as soon as I was back on the market not a soul appeared to be interested. When I was a man who was taken, the women were flocking by the dozen.

I'm going to share this secret with my men readers while it's on my mind. Find you a beautiful woman friend take her out with you, time to time I bet you will pull the baddest woman in the place. I'm not saying all women so don't quote me, but most women love competition. When a woman catches sight of a man with an eye-catching woman, his attraction level will increase. Trust me when I say this fellas, it works!

Thursday night I decided to step out for the first time since I moved into my apartment. Earlier in the day, Shawn my slick wrist barber awarded me with a razor shape polished haircut; so, I was formerly infatuated with myself. When I threw Jeans and a top on with a pair of white Ones and sprayed cologne on my neck and wrist at that moment, I felt good about myself for the first time in a long time. I glanced in the body mirror boosting the author up

"You're Tink, you are one handsome man." I said, internally I was nervous to escape those four walls, "it's been a long time since I've stepped alone as a single man," I hyped myself up some more. "You are Tink, you're the man!" I beat my chest with a balled fist before leaving the apartment.

I went to a lounge on the west end of Pittsburgh. Frogs was not a place I normally would prefer to hang out at because the people who are usually there are sometimes weird. You would find a couple beautiful flamingos but the rest of the women would be frogs and ducks. (That's my opinion) Frogs was more of a low-key spot to attend than going to a busy establishment like Arts Bar in the midtown of Pittsburgh. I was not psychologically prepared to be around a crowded scene, even though this night at Frogs was semi-filled. There were a ton of parked vehicles on the busy street, therefore I parked two blocked down from Frogs.

Inside of the lounge, this place was jumping; all the seats around the bar were taken, the side tables were occupied; but luckily for me, a couple removed themselves from two of the bar stools then went to separate side of Frog's where there was a dance floor, a DJ and a bar as well. Tonight, the beautiful flamingos were out and so were the ducks. It was wing night plus it was the second to last day of the work night. At this time, I rarely drank for a substitute I ordered two glasses of chardonnay dry, red wine and sat at the bar pretending to watch the Lakers vs Gold State game as I periodically checked my phone. No mentions or text messages, my phone was as dry as the wine.

Sitting alone I felt like an outsider, I had no one to speak to. In my mind, I was the awkward guy in the bar gazing at women walking past. I knew deep down when a man gives the impression of being thirsty the women would pay the man no type of attention. They would see you as a creep.

If you're sightseeing and happen to get a woman to eyeball you in return, follow the three-second rule. You have three seconds to approach that woman. You've got eye contact with her. If not, the longer you stare and smile, stare and smile or even wave; 9 times out of 10 she'll think you're strange. This is where I fucked up because sitting five stools beside me, there were two women. One was drop-dead gorgeous, hazel completion with beautiful full lips and had stormy gray hair. She looked me dead in the eyes and shot me a smile. I beamed back reviling my gap then rapidly I turned my attention to the television screen across the bar. No doubt, my insides were quivering and my ass was glued to my seat. The conscience in my mind was over speaking the music in Frogs. "What if she gives you the cold shoulder? What are you going to say when you approach her? What if she has a boyfriend? You're about to make yourself look like a fool." The confidence I once had four years ago before getting into a long-term relationship was outright out the window and all the chest-beating and gassing myself up before entering Frog's deflated; I was terrified.

"Want another glass of wine." The bartender asked. Either she knew I was panicky or she felt bad that I was sitting alone.

"Yes. What I owe you." I replied

"Someone bought you a drink." The snow-white bartender said then scrambled around the bar to pour drinks. I caught sight of Stormy again; this time her friend was not sitting with her. This was my opportunity to prove myself wrong.

"You got this, you got this."

Stormy was occupied with her phone. She probably felt me burning a hole in her neck with my eyes.

"Go Tink, Go, you got this." I pushed myself some more as the bartender sat my wine on a napkin.

"Thank you, and please tell whoever bought this for me thank you."
"I will." As soon as the bartender disappeared, my left foot tapped the ground.

"I can do this," I spoke to myself. Right as both rubbers of my soles touched the surface, the friend appeared, Stormy stood up from her chair, grasped her belongings they began to stroll towards the exit. Before their departure, she waved then vanished out the door. I allowed my self-esteem to get in the way; I allowed rejection to put fear in my heart. I allowed my thoughts to cloud my mind with negative. At this time, I knew I had to work on myself.

Soon after Stormy left my confidence was at an all-time low, I could not stay in Frogs for another second. Leaving the lounge my vehicle was parked quite a distance; I had three glasses of wine as a result I was sort of intoxicated. I noticed someone was four to five feet away from me walking in the same direction. I didn't see any harm in this guy so I didn't consider closely because there were other vehicles parked behind mine. When I stepped inside my car the man following behind me opened the passenger door.

"Hey, I bought you those drinks."
"Ah If you don't shut my fucking door, I'mma shot you," I said reaching under my seat.
"I just want to suck your dick." He said stepping back in fear, after slamming my door.
When I pulled off, I shed tears the whole drive home. AT THIS TIME, I WAS ABSOLUTELY AT MY WORST.

Like most movies when hard times occur, the script usually has the main character revisit their past. Say a character could not reach his goal because something ruined his master plan. The character was near success but fell short; so, he gets depressed then comes to a conclusion to land at his old job, the place where he absolutely despised. I was that character at the time, I wanted my ex-fiancé back. The next morning, I sent a text through messages and it read:

"Good morning. Hey, we should get a workout in; take a jog at the reservoir or something." I knew she was a health freak. The scheme was to give attention to her interests without displaying desperation or the hurt that's tattooed on the beating heart. At the core of it all; I wasn't going to beg or discuss the dead and buried.

When you beg, your weakness will be exposed. Most of the time when this happens you'll get shut down swiftly. Your feeling will be unquestionably damaged and your heart will get Kirk Franklin stomped. Just enjoy yourself, allow the energy to flow naturally between you both, and don't overly bend over backward because you'll seem like a fraud and resemble a goofball. When it comes down to winning back your old lady just be yourself. Be consistent, do the shit you'd say you would do but don't bug her every day with the "what you doing? Can I see you?" texts. She's still in the healing process; give her the space; even after you too lived it up. Slightly fall back and compel her to miss your presence.

Surprisingly she agreed, we planned to go running the very next day. Wednesday evening, it was a beautiful spring day; people were jogging, riding bikes, skating, walking, and walking their dogs, families with children, and elderlies pacing around cherishing the weather. A lap around the reservoir was a full mile, we jogged around twice and the third one we walked. As we took our last stroll we exchanged small talk conversations, plans for our child, business plans, and a whole lot of nothing. When we finished walking the mile, I escort her to the car.

"I know who she is, you did fuck her Darren."
"No I didn't." was my lying response
"Well, Roland said you told him you did. He has no reason to lie."
"I never said nothing to him about nobody. They just don't want to us together because they're having problems in their relationship."

Roland was my ex-fiancée's friend's husband; we became close friends within the four years of my relationship. During the football season, we watched Steeler games on Sundays, attended a few bitterly cold weather games, exchanged businesses plans, and went on double dates in and out of town with our ladies. Other than my brother Devon or my childhood friends Wade or Carlos the solid men I would trust with my life; Roland was the friend who I was building trust with. Since we both were in a relationship, the conversations were different than talking to my single friends. When we spoke, it was similar to visiting a therapist. If I had any issues at home in my relationship he was the person I called to vent to and vice versa. He spoke on a ton of dilemmas he had with his lady or outside deceiving shit, he'd brought to a conclusion. As a man, my mouth will be forever concealed and his words will always be locked in my soul even if we're not friends. My mistake was believing that the guy code was obeyed by every man.

After getting caught; a week later Roland and I gave a voice on the entanglement on his living room sofa. I exposed the view of the woman's Instagram page, I described the sexual act between the woman and I and I clarified the reason for the actions on my part. When I reflect on bragging about a woman I slept with; that is the corniest shit I could've done. Apart from getting caught, this unmanly behavior cause by boasting about new pussy caused me fully. Never tell a married man or a man deep in a relationship your infidelities. These men are known for pillow talking. All the info shared was passed over to his woman then to my ex. The guy code was thoroughly broken. There was no chance of myself getting back in good hands. She knew the full story added to that there was a face to paint the picture clearly.

After the day, we jogged two weeks later; I invited the ex-fiancée to a DC Young Fly comedy show for her birthday. The night was flourishing we both were dressed prevailing and DC Young Fly had us rolling out of our seats with joke after jokes. A good laugh purposely brings the tension out of the situation. When the show was over, I dropped her off and picked our child up while she went out for her birthday. It was a Friday night and Saturday mornings I had to attend work a 5 am so I had to drop my child off whenever she arrived home. At 1am, again she mentioned Cassidy.

"I was in the car talking to Tasha and we called Roland, he said you fucked that girl." This time I felt Roland gave full details, straight from his lips.
"Why are we talking about this again, I thought we're past this."
"We're not, you want me to call him."
"For what?" I said as her phone rang on speaker.
"Hello," Roland answered his phone.
"Hey, Roland. Did Darren fuck that girl?" she asked, staring me down.

"YUP," he said without a care; she hung the phone up.

"Just leave me alone. The only way you can get me back with me; you have to stop writing, give me your passwords and give me a key to your apartment." None of those options was happening so it was over. It was time to return to the drawing board.

.

003.The Peeling Process

Once I knew the window of opportunity to reunite with my ex-fiancé was closed, a wave of feelings left my spirit; I no longer had care in my bones. This was the same emotion I felt when my first love in high school fucked my neighbor across the street. Sixteen years old I was on the edge of the bed with alligator tears streaming down my young face. My heart was vastly crushed, I felt abandoned, misled, and defeated. I hated life I hated everyone. I didn't want to live anymore. Then something shook my consciousness; something smacked me in the face like a bag of bricks. On each brick in the bag had a short quote, which changed my life for a long period. "Never trust another woman, I will never be in this position again, I will never open up to another woman, fuck these hoes, I don't give a fuck anymore." At that moment, a whole new beast was developed; this was the beginning of the savage life. Multiple women at once, the nonchalant attitude, the cheating, the mind games, and the manipulation. Every drop of trust and love was squeezed out of my heart like a lemon. I now had a black heart.

These same thoughts resurfaced seventeen years later. I had been out of commission for four years, but I had to move more fashionable this time around. The first step was finding myself, loving who I was, and having a deep relationship with the inner me before allowing anyone into my space. As I endured the peeling process, I had to invest in me before dealing with other women.

The practice I used to reintroduce myself to live a happier and stress-free lifestyle, every morning I would listen to motivational speakers on YouTube; Here are a few names of my choosing, "Les Brown, Eric Thomas, Jim Rohn, and Earl Nightingale." (Address your ability to read books yet listen to audiobooks during your spare time. Why? So, the reader can appreciate the authors liken to other books.) As a writer, I barely have time to read so for an alternative I listen to audiobooks when I drive or traveling in the air. Jen Sincro's "You Are A Badass", Gary John Bishop's "Unfuck Yourself" was another good book. I probably listened to 30 books in the past two years. I discovered meditation and manifesting, I began to pray more often; I took hot spiritual baths with candle lights and pleasantly smooth music. I wrote down my thoughts and goals in journals, embraced my body; ate clean and exercised, had conversations with myself in the mirrors, and complimented myself in many ways. I did not allow the outer world to disturb my inner peace; I canceled all the bad thoughts and knew good would happen for me even if my day was not the greatest. The most therapeutic task was decorating my apartment, going to the home store buying plants, lamps with warm light bulbs, candles, adjustment color strip lights, canvas photos, rugs, and furniture to bring the place a vibe and comfortability was everything. You live a messy life and life will be messy.

(Hint: to the guys reading this book going through the peeling process. When your place is, polished, and decorated to amazement; the first question a woman will ask is "Did one of your girls help you decorate?" Next thing it is ten times easier to get some pussy when your place is laid out. Best to have warm lights to bring a relaxing environment. You want them to feel homely. Another fact about candlelight and warm lights is when a woman glares in your eyes, your gaze will be engaging. She'll think you're looking into her soul. Always play smooth music to match the mood as well. Bright lights will kill the setting and so will a dirty ass house with sheets on the windows as curtains.

Be careful what you manifest. After Roland blew up my cover by breaking the guy code and I decided to get in tune with myself. I was geared to date again. Even though I fell in love with myself, I still was lonely. Out of desperation, I manifested to have an abundance of women. Instead of manifesting generational wealth or a better lifestyle out of all things. My manifestation was women. What in the fuck was I thinking? I got exactly what I asked for, this same day I posted a nice photo on Instagram. Five women reached out to me in my messages; two newbies and three girls I had fucked in the past. It was funny how exes and old tails shoot their shot when sharing a handsome photo of myself. Within a month, I laid down with three out of the five ladies who messaged me. That same day at wholefoods, I exchanged numbers with a beautiful big booty coffee-colored woman behind the register who I eventually fucked two days later. That same Thursday night I went to 'The Spot' a bar in Penn Hills an urban-suburban area 20 minutes from Downtown Pittsburgh.

It was the end of June of 2019 and it was before COVID and wearing the mask. This bar was jumping; this was an environment I was beyond familiar with because I was born and raised on the east side of Pittsburgh so I knew a good number of people. The bar was congested with men and women waving money to get the bartender's attention, others socialized from one corner to the other side of the room.

With all the attention, I received all in one day my confidence was at its peak. Shot down or not I was in a savage mood. Once a woman laid eyes on me three seconds later I was approaching them without shaking a bone in my body. I was back to my little boy ways but this time I was a grown-ass man. Out of all the numbers, I accumulated this night there was one woman that struck my interest the most. I'm a sucker for women with color in their hair such as grey, blonde, pink, green, and especially red or burgundy. I learned to not compliment women when speaking to them or starting a conversation with "what's up beautiful or hey cutie what's your name or what are you drinking tonight?" These are the same lame-ass pickup lines that mostly every man says on the daily. Women are bored with the same shit being thrown at them; look around find something else to talk about other than her looks. Just be creative. I'm not sure if I wrote this somewhere in the book yet or not but women despite being called "Sexy" I wrote this quote on Instagram here are a few comments my lady followers said: @everybody_hates_nik "yes! Hate it, complete turn-off." @kali_allthighs "I thought I was the only one who hated being called that. Here are a few more out of 100 comments @jayquelynn80 "Amen to that. Try something different. This guy made me smile the other day, he came to me and said I like your glasses and started a convo that way." @kinleyydanielle "They don't understand." Over 800 women liked this post; so, the fact is leave the word "Sexy" out of your vocabulary when speaking to a woman.

This particular woman I was deeply attracted to her. She had Wendy's red hair, a sugar brown skin tone, her eyes were dreamy which matched her gorgeous smile. I was sitting diagonally from her at the bar; I noticed there was a vacant seat beside her and the friend she was engaged in a conversation with. The redhead woman hadn't gazed in my direction not once so this was a cold turkey approach; it was all a plot. Most cold-turkey approaches can be awkward, never tap on a woman's shoulder or rudely speak to her while she's in the middle of a conversation. Since I was not on her radar I played music chairs, I stood from my chair then I walked over to the empty chair beside her. Since the friend was facing towards the direction I was standing, I got eye contact with the friend instead of the redhead target.

"Excuse me, anyone sitting here." The target and the friend turned their attention to me.

"No." the friend said. The friend was cute as well. I thought to myself.

"No. I don't think so." Redhead responded seconds off from unison.

"Do, you mind if I sit here?" I asked kindly.

"No, we don't mind." The redhead answered then resumed back to their conversation.

I ordered cheese fries and a glass of wine. It was a cheat meal. Within ten minutes of sitting beside the ladies, the redhead friend stood up out of the seat then disappeared into the crowd. This is when the opportunity presented itself; she was sitting alone. The bartender came toward our way and planted food in front of redhead.

"How long did it take for your food to come?" I asked breaking the ice.

"We been waiting for almost 30 minutes."

"Guess I have some time to wait."

"30 minutes isn't long." She said holding a cracked screen iPhone with a photo of a child delayed on the screensaver.

"Wow, that little girl looks exactly like you."

"Yes, that's my twin."

"Clearly. What's your name?" I asked.

"Vanessa." I reached for her hand and noticed the glossy orange manicure, her fingernails were about 3 inches long except for the index finger that appeared chewed up.

"My name is Tink or Tinker, nice to meet you." I grasped her hand to embrace.

Sometimes it's best to get straight to the point when talking to a woman. The reason I say this is because some men will talk too much about nothing, show their corny side or lose words to say, when there's nothing else to talk about then the shit can get awkward. Then there are the men with radical and alluring personalities, who can hold an interesting lengthy conversation. For the men who are not as outgoing as others, shoot your shot ask for a date, get the number then disappear. This is exactly what I did at that moment.

"We should let me take you out for tacos one of these days." Ninety percent of women love tacos, might be a fact but tacos or ice cream always win for me.

"Are you sure you want to take me out? I'm crazy."

"I'm probably as crazy as you. What's your number?" We exchanged numbers just in time as her friend came back on the scene.

A week later, in the text message, Vanessa mentioned she worked at a hospital on the North Side, which was approximately five minutes away from where I stayed. This day I happened to get off work earlier than usual so I invited her over for brunch. While we were texting back and forth, I was previously in the kitchen cooking wholegrain protein cinnamon pancakes, scrambled eggs with spinach, turkey sausage, and sweet potato home fries. I sent her the address then within fifteen minutes, she was at my door. I sat the adjustable food trays in my bedroom and we scraped plates with forks in the time a movie on Amazon Prime played on the television. Have you ever met someone that is exceedingly talkative and overly animated? This was Vanessa, I didn't have to speak much, one question here and there then she will take the stage; all I did was nod my head to agree or shake my head to disagree. "Dang, wow, that's crazy." That was what I mumbled the entire afternoon for the period I listened to Vanessa ramble. When her break ended she asked to come back later after she'd worked. I didn't mind.

"I'll come back over as soon as I get off." She declared

"What time you get off?"

"4:30"

4:30 passed, I did not text or call to figure out if she was coming or not. If she wanted to spend time with me she would have contacted me. What a woman does not like is a pest. It's okay to text once. I could've texted "Hey are we still on for 4:30?" If you don't get a reply back please do not double text. Especially clocking them asking, "Where are you? It's 4:30."

If she or anyone doesn't respect your time, it's a big FUCK YOU. If I'm busy after the time we planned, then you missed out on your opportunity to be around my greatness. I had options of women that I could have called; within a snap of a finger, one of them would've been on their way. I did not want to waste my energy; instead, I ordered Nicky's Thai food and watched the Netflix series "All American."

7:30 something PM

"What you doing? I went to Happy Hour with a friend that works with me." Vanessa texted, I didn't bash her for being unsympathetic. There was no need to be in my feelings over a text, phone call, or even in person but I would address how I felt about how important my time was when she was with me.

"Watching a show on Netflix."

"Can I still come over?"

"Maybe, another day." That was what I should've texted but I knew once she was in possession, she would be an effortless fuck.

"Yes." My dick mind shot a signaled to my thumb to type.

"I'm about to leave now."

8:00 something PM

She came in my place smelling like a bar, the alcohol reeked from her mouth but she appeared sober. She spoke proper without stumbling over words or falling all over the place. I directed Vanessa through the living room, the hallway into the bedroom. Outside the windows daylight was turning to night, the television was the main source of light in the room. Since she had been out all day, I offered her basketball shorts and a t-shirt. I'm a slight germaphobe; I won't allow anyone to lay on the sheets with outside clothes on. She denied the hoop shorts but wore the t-shirt. In minutes, she laid beside me and watched a few minutes of the Netflix episode. She placed her redhead on my chest while I held her in my arms as if I knew her for some years. Planting kisses on her forehead and firmly rubbing my fingers against the muscles of her mid-back, she snuggled me tightly. The show was irrelevant; at this point, the television was just background noise to get us started. I pecked soft kisses on her forehead some more. She turned her face upwards and laid her eyes on mine, our faces leaned, in unison. Our lips brushed twice, a split second after, our tongues slithered against one another. With my free hand that wasn't concealed under Vanessa's body, I clinched my palm around her throat like a turtleneck then pulled in for deeper kisses. As my tongue snaked down this woman's tonsils, her body quivered while moans escaped between her lips. While we continued to exchange saliva, I released my hand from her throat and reached between Vanessa's thighs then applied my index and middle fingers against the thin wet fabric of her panties that layered over her love box. When locating the clit, I leisurely massaged the button in a circular rotary motion. Her moans escalated a bit and her panties were beyond soaked.

As much as I have a passion for eating the kitty I was on the fence of should I or shouldn't I.

I scooted my arm from under Vanessa to free myself then perched my body over her frame. I pressed my lips lightly on her neck then trailed wet lip blots down her collar then down to the chest where I compassed a pit stop. Like a breastfeeding baby, I wrapped my mouth around her nipple then grabbed hold of the other 32C breast as I began to glide my tongue for no longer than a minute. I crossed over to the opposite titty, giving the same tongue treatment except on this occasion I was caressing her drenched pussy with the two front line fingers. Stimulating the clit, I rubbed directly against it to build her fire of desire for me and what I had to offer. Her midsection thrust up and down on the mattress as she wailed from each swab. My fingers were supremely slippery and I could not help but duck low to the central location. In no time, I was feasting on the pussy. Her legs were spread apart and her feet were grounded, creating a dent in the mattress. The tip of my tongue slapped the clit continually, saliva and her natural liquids were spilling out my mouth as gripped her securely beneath her butter-soft slim thick ass and lifted like an empty bowl of cereal with just milk.

"Yes. Tink yes…Tink." she moaned giving sexual vibrations. (Ladies: When a man is amused and turned on while eating your box. He's a pleaser.)

"I'm cumin. I'm cumin." She said the magic words. I licked, licked, and licked as she shifted her waist up and down until her body stiffened and released her soul all over my mouthpiece.

This eight-inch black thickness was solid with a hook; she wrapped her mouth around my manhood for literately a half a minute.

"Lay back," I demanded, pushing her back by the throat. Probably biting my bottom lip.

I gradually plugged myself between her open thighs, she was gasping for air as I inched my way deeper with each stroke I delivered. I pushed my hips to the bottom at a ponderous pace to get her accustomed to the dick. I penetrate on my knees glaring down at this redhead woman devoting her entire body to me. Instead of beating the kitty at the opening drive, I wanted to get a feel for her body. Vanessa's muffin was warm like a baked sweet potato.

I laid over top, chest on chest, and whipped my backside with a bit more force striking at a mid-pace. Her moans were now in high definition with my ears just centimeters from her voice box. Once she fully adapted and we aligned with one another this was when the connection got deeper and the energy become a sexual force. She didn't lay there like a dead fish by just taking the penetration; she fucked back. When I thrust in she heaved up while she held her hands around my neck. Our ebony skins slapped, the bed swayed, curse words expressions, my shit-talking, her moans, the multiple orgasms she let off, and the heavy breathing; the exchange of energy thunderous filled the room. After a good 40 minutes to an hour, we finished.

Two months, Vanessa and I spent a ton of time together while I juggled other women in-between time. Family gatherings, dates, sleepovers; as time went on we began to develop feelings for one another but I was not psyched up for a new relationship. So unexpectedly, I went ghost; the more she grew closer to me the more I stepped back. When the feelings got deeper I was all out. This was when the shit hit the fan. It was crazy like 100 blocked calls a day, threatening voice mails, text message after text, once I blocked the number she texted from a different number. On top of that, the other women were getting frustrated because I was not spending time with them during the days I gave Vanessa my attention. Remember when Vanessa said she was crazy when I met her? Until this day, if a woman tells me she's crazy. I will leave here where she's at.

NOTE FOR CHAPTER 3:

Be mindful of what you manifest, you might get what you deserve in the worst way. Manifesting an abundance of women is just a mixture of spirits. It's like picking raffle tickets out of a box; you just don't know what you'll get. This might be the realest quote in the book but after a year of dealing with a ton of women, you'll notice your soul is rotten. Deep down inside there is pain.

An old head told me; "Out of all the women you sleeping with one of them could have been a wife. You probably missed out on a good woman because you did not take the time to get to know who she can be. All you wanted was to get your dick wet."

Intermission Poem I wrote January 28th, 2020

Graffiti written on the wall in the safe place of the bathroom.

Peeing in a toilet full of cigarette butts, brown paper towel, wasted alcohol and a slice of lime. As I stand on the urinated floor, my mind is twisted from countless sipping. Vibrations of hip-hop bass rattled the ground through the closed door. I cleanse my hands then stare in the mirror at this handsome face. In these brown eyes, there is pain overlaid by an abundance of women. Nightlife in this congested club I discern vacant hearts from the opposite sex that I will fill with my charm and courage. Once a divine woman set eyes on me; someone's daughter is getting chosen. A smile displays my dimple and an approach that exhibits certainty;

creates conversation and sometimes followed by drinks. That leads to a phone number or a one-way ticket to my place. Neck chokes and deep kissing to expelling our clothes. The melanin in our bodies attach, moans escape through her lips as I sway my hips in her water grips. Each stroke I deliver is ripping a scab from my wounded heart. Not allowing myself to heal, I'm burying all my pain inside this woman's ovaries as she climaxes all over my shaft. The feelings I once had for this woman instantly decrease when I release this misery over her chest.

Peeling the scab off my heart

Juggling hearts, lifting souls and giving orgasms away like turkeys on Thanksgiving. I'm turning my back on love. Now I have a variety of women. Scabs from the heart are peeling each time I'm penetrating between open thighs. When will, I open my eyes that I'm not healing, it's just a temporary feeling. Lust can fade away like dust on a windy day. I admire big butts and a pretty face, I might cut then throw away. Swimming in women but I'm still lonely, no matter what I do; these women still want me. Can't dwell on the past but yet it still haunts me. A broken glass vase can be repaired but it will never be the same, peeling scabs off the heart when I'm rocking bed frames. She tells me it's yours, all I can say is cum on it. Choke her from behind while I arch her back, don't run from it. She's grasping sheets, moans from granite teeth, as she takes my pain as I constantly slide deep. Would I ever love again? Only time will tell.

Drowning in women makes it hard to find myself. Ripping scabs from my heart, I have no time to heal.

Peeling the scab off my heart

Tinker Jeffries

004. Pride

Pride, Pride can build you or it can break you.

In 2005, I lived in Greenspoint, Houston Texas where I attended an automotive trade school. I spent mornings at school and evenings at Walmart in the tire and lube department where I became a certified lube technician. At this time of my life, I was fresh out of high school and I just turned twenty. It was the life checking out a new city 1,300 miles away from home. I was a woman savage to the core; I wouldn't allow a woman I thought was appealing to pass my direction. It did not matter if you were my age or fifty years old, if I had a desire for you I was speaking.

Working at Walmart I met the woman who altered my entire life. She was getting new tires or getting her oil and filter changed; I don't recollect the service she got on the vehicle but I remember the lime green velour sweatsuit she wore and deep southern New Orleans accent. She had hazel brown eyes, 5'8" long legs, she has some desirable facial features, high cheekbones, and a bright big beautiful smile. Her hair was in micro braids because that was the style in the early 2000s. She was fine, fine. My position on the job was to write the tickets for the customers when they pulled up to the bay. It took everything to remember what I was doing after spotting her, I had to tell myself, *check the mileage, and get their personal information.*

Under the hood I had to inspect the fluid levels and air filters; basically, the angle was to sell a new air filter and convince the customer into upgrading to synthetic oil. While I'm inspecting, this nice-looking woman sat in the white Toyota Camry, I behaved in a playful matter, saying goofy lines to make her laugh. As I'm completing the ticket, I notice the license plate had four letters and three numbers, which read

412. That would be my starting point as that was the Pittsburgh area code. The three-second rule to speak to a woman was not in my play at this age, she was so athletic I couldn't gather the words to utter. I froze and allowed her to slip away into the store. While she was shopping in Walmart, I was granted time to thaw out and build confidence. She was out of my league, for one I'm making eight dollars an hour getting approximately $450 bi-weekly to be a grease monkey. I was a struggling student nearly eating Ramen Noodles and Toni's Frozen Pizza daily, I didn't have a vehicle, and the public buses ran once an hour. The solo plus was that I had an apartment. Other than a place to live what the fuck could I bring to the table? Absolutely nothing! I made it clear to myself when she came to get the Toyota I would be on her like butter on bread. That I did! I was in the bay talking to a co-worker when I witnessed the fine Toyota owner coming out the swinging gray metal doors and walking towards the lot that we parked the finished cars. By the time I caught up to her she was flopping down into the driver's seat.

"Excuse me," I said a slight jittery, not enough to display my nervousness. She turned her attention in my direction and reached for the door handle.

"Yes."

"I just couldn't let you leave without saying something." She glanced at me halfhearted with squinting eyes and a smirk.

"Oh huh, honey. How old are you?

"20" I responded.

"Oh no, You're a Juve; Baby. You must want me in jail." She voiced in her deep New Orleans accent.

"That don't mean nothing. How old are you?" I asked while I felt like I was shrinking each second I spoke.

"I'm old; baby. A little too old for you." She seemed as she was thrilled to call me young.

"I may be young but my youth will expand your life."
"Oh, is that right." She chuckled.
"Yes. You didn't know that."
"You're cute with your little lines. What's your name?"
"Tink. What's your name?"
"They call me Slim, but It's Lamara. Take my number."

A month went by; we went on a date and talked on the phone for hours throughout the 30 days. We didn't spend as much time together because she had her child the majority of the time. New Orleans was quite damaged on the grounds of the ferocious Hurricane Katrina so Lamara's family was scattered in different cities. Finding a trustworthy sitter was difficult for the fact that she did not know anyone. Lamara left town for some days then came back kid-free. The day I was invited over to her place altered my life forever. I felt like she placed a New Orleans curse on me; though I did not notice any signs of witchcraft.

It was a Friday evening and I was supposed to be at work at 4:00PM. This was my first time stepping foot into Lamara's house. Rather than going to work, I called off pretending to be sick. My priorities as a young man were unacceptable. Eventually, I got fired.

"Don't worry, about coming back." The supervisor Mike declared. Word of advice: money over pleasure, but in the long run me getting fired to be with Lamara was well worth it. She is one of the reasons why I can write erotic books.
It all started with a kiss while sitting on the couch. A soft intimate peck, which turned into our tongues intertwining together. She was wearing a white spaghetti strap tank top and had nice plump c cup breasts. I placed kisses on her neck as I pulled the strings on the tank top down her shoulders then I snapped the back of the bra with a finger snap. That was some shit that I learned in high school.

I painted each nipple with my tongue then went straight for the kill. I unbuttoned Lamara's pants, slid her jeans down her cinnamon long legs, slid the panties off then stuffed my face in between her thighs. My tongue slithered in all directions with no accuracy of stimulating the clit, I was oblivious of my oral performance. In my regards, I was masterful at eating the box, not a soul complained in the short four years of snacking at the downstairs restaurant. I was on my knees on the wooden floor and my tongue was whipping all over the place, just licking, licking, and licking. Lamara's moans echoed throughout the room for a short amount of time then the moans died down when I paused or began to stroke my tongue elsewhere.

"Hold on honey," She said reaching her labia (Pussy Lips) and spread them apart with the index and middle fingers of both hands; exposing the clitoris, which resembled a jellybean.

"Lick right here, make your mouth wet, and suck but not too hard." She instructed as she guided the back of her head toward the button. I didn't allow my pride to get in the way; I followed her guidelines and began sweeping my taste buds against the pearl, as I slightly slurped. Overanalyzing her instructions and determined to make her climax I became apprehensive. I kept glaring up to observe her reacting. I caught her gazing down with eyes wide open. I also viewed her with shut eyes. I did not notice that I was tense but she felt I was stiff as a board.

"Relax baby, relax. Breathe out your nose." She said in that accent. When the word "relax" spilled out her lips, straight away I felt the tension. My body deflated as soon as I was mindful that I overthinking and doing too much. At this moment I closed my eyes and permitted my tongue to be the vision that stimulated the clit, I tuned out all background noises and listened to the patterns of her breathing in unison with the moans, I constantly slid my tongue back and forth while I inhaled and exhaled out of my nostrils. It felt like mediating while eating pussy. I didn't know nothing about meditation at twenty. I felt her stomach sinking in, she began breathing deeply, her body started to tremble then into the time she let loose all the frustration over my lips as her body collapsed.

NOTE:

1. While you're eating your woman; sucking and licking on the clit. Grasp her by the waist then pull her body into your face in unison as you continue to lick and suck. It's like she's penetrating your face, she can feel that collision against your lips when you pull her in.
2. Have you ever seen a fish move its mouth? If not google it. Again, when you're licking and sucking, move your lips as if you're a fish. This skill allows the upper lip to stimulate the outside of the clitoris hood.
3. For those with gap teeth like I, when eating the pussy, you can suck air in between your front teeth to allow a cool breeze to draft against the clit. A lot of women love this technique but I came across some that couldn't handle the chill.
4. Note: Some women do not like fingers stuck in them but most do. So, this technique is the cheat code to make a woman cum. While you're eating your woman. Plug your finger inside; make sure your nails are cut and clean. Turn your hand to the palm; curl your index and middle finger towards the beginning of her upper wall, which feels like a sponge. As you lick against the clit, rub that sponge until she melts all over your hand.
5. Like Lamara said in the story "Relax." A woman can feel when you're tense. She can feel when you're not comfortable or you're doing too much to please her. When you're not at ease she's not as well, which makes it more challenging to cum.

6. Simple: Listen to your woman. She knows what she likes. After a while, you will know your lady's body. Pay attention to her body rhythm, the way she breathes, moans, and her body motion. Is her hand somewhere random, is her stomach sinking in and out?

"Come on, up here," Lamara said glaring at me with an arousing spark in her eyes. I got up from the wooden floor then hung over her naked soul, our tongues reunited as I slid my basketball shorts halfway down my thighs. In the seam of Lamara's long legs, I grasp hold of my erupted 8-inch midnight black hook then plug myself, in moderation. The excitement, the anticipating, the moment I couldn't believe I was into the wet interior of this alluring woman. The second I gained access, I went ballistic. Literality ballistic. I did hard long strokes putting all my back in her with a motionless blistering pace. She expressed a sprinkle of moans that was enough to inform that I was pleasing her while I penetrated; probably making the most passionate pleasuring facial expression. Abruptly I felt her palm on my chest.

"Stop, stop! What are you doing?" Lamara said in an unsatisfying tone. I was unable to say a word; in my mind, I thought I was giving her the business. Unfortunately, the business was shut down. I lost my virginity the day before I became thirteen, had sex through middle school and a ton in high school, got to college, and slept with a few women in Texas. Now all of a sudden I was getting questioned about sex by a woman that was eight years older than I was. No one in the past complained, why Lamara?

"You're just fucking, you're not worrying about how I'm feeling. Slow it down get a feel for me." She instructed. "Okay," I voiced like a sad child then began to stroke in an unhurried pace.

"Use your hips. Not your back." She said pressing down on my waistline. Figuring out to just stroke with my midsection was like rubbing my stomach in a circular motion and patting my head in unison. I couldn't put an end to using my back.

"Look baby, just swing your hips." She guided my waist steadily.

"Yes, keep swinging. Align your body with mines, do you feel me lifting up?" she continued coaching, her ass lifted and fell in and out the couch cushion. When she rose I shifted in, when she fell, I shifted out in sequence. Once I established a rhythm of swaying my waist and became acquainted with incorporating not just my needs but Lamara's desires as well, that's when I got the picture. Intercourse wasn't a selfish deed especially if you had intentions on dating someone for a long period. When the man is determined to fulfill all her sexual necessities and she in the same boat to do so likewise the sex will be beyond epic like the grand finale on the Fourth of July. The heavy heart beating, toe-curling, sheet gripping, soul connecting out-of-body experiences of orgasms lift both spirits when everyone is looking out for each other.

Unfortunately, for Lamara there wasn't any spirit-lifting for her. Within ten minutes you know what happened. Yes, I blew it, I blew it big time. The love box felt so pleasant I couldn't hold back. I let loose filling the condom with my good graces. I assumed Lamara understood I was young and inexperienced, after this moment we still had a lovely friendship but I never had a chance to redeem myself.

This experience taught me enough, but I was yearning to absorb furthermore in respect of pleasing women. I read magazines with sex tips like Men's Health and GQ. I read books and watched a ton of porn, not to get off but to take notes. Back in the early two thousands, my favorites porn stars were Jada Fire, Cherokee, and Roxy Reynolds. As I absorbed all the knowledge while being sexually active, I began to notice the difference in the way women were acting after our sexual encounters. Some became clingy, some craved sex and were super demanding, some became delusional; assuming we were a relationship, some became crazy and some just knew if we continued to sleep around the feelings would get deep; so, they ran away to protect their heart. Once a man learns how to read a woman's body, he becomes dangerous in the bedroom or any unpredicted place you and the significant other have the urge to fuck at. The most important point I learned about sex, is that you two have to be mentally connected first unless he or she is fucking for a different purpose other than fondness.

005. Followers

July 2009 East Liberty, Pittsburgh Pa. 24-25 years old.

    At this time in my life, I had high beliefs about becoming a rapper. So, I invested thousands of dollars in creating music and visuals. I paid four hundred to five hundred dollars for music videos directed by Jordan Beckham and two hundred to three hundred dollars for studio time. I had ideas of creating a reality blog for YouTube so I bought a hundred-dollar video camera. The first day I had the video camera I goofed around and recorded a how-to video but not your typical cooking recipe, builder, or fix a car tutorial video. I recorded a tutorial on eating the box. If you search "Tinker Jeffries How to Eat Pussy Part 1" on YouTube it will appear. This video has 103k views and probably a million more after this book is published. Tons of blessings came out of this recording even though I can't stand the way I was talking. A woman discovered me on YouTube, searched me on Facebook then messaged me. We hit it off twice with a condom, the second time the rubber broke then Boom! I was blessed with a beautiful child. The downside of this situation was I did not know anything about this woman. To this day I still don't know the mother's age.

This video allowed me to serve others. If I had a dollar for every straight man or lesbian woman who said "thank you" I would be rich. This video brought a stream of attention to my social media and random people would ask sex questions for guidance.

A Few questions from followers:

(Woman) Question: What does it do for a guy when a woman swallows his cum? I mean I agree to suck until he explodes of course but why swallow it? I never understood why that excites guys.

Answer: It's all mental for us. A man loves when his woman goes above and beyond her seductive level.

(Woman) Question: So, I use to be able to give mind-blowing oral sex. I think I've got boring cause it takes longer for my fiancé to nut. What can I do?

Answer: I'm going to assume that you use your hands while giving him head because most women do. Undertake other ways in oral, like massaging his balls gently with wet fingers as you suck, lick around the cone of the penis which is called edging; this right here could be a tease but it feels amazing. When it's time for you to give him oral, it may be easier for him to cum because he'll be fully aroused. Let him stroke his own dick after you have sucked him for a while; open your mouth and slid your tongue across the head. Use a ton of saliva to keep his pipe moist because sometimes masturbating can get dry. Moan throughout the whole time. When a man senses that a woman is taking pleasure in sucking his dick in his mind, he'll have thoughts of her being nasty just for him. You're his personal whore.

(Male) Question: I been with my girlfriend for a year and a half, at the beginning we had sex 3 to 4 times a week to once a week, sometimes none. How do I explain to her that I need more sex?

Answer: Sexual attention sometimes gets lost because of the change of lifestyle, boredom, not being excited about the same routine of sex, for some a kid get involved, or she's not feeling you anymore. This is my personal opinion, instead of talking about what you need sexually add some spice into your relationship. Have a date night once a week to reconnect mentally. Have spontaneous sex; fuck her in the parking lot, in the car in front of the house, on the elevator, or just in a different environment from the norm. At home, give massages, rub her feet, and back the entire body. Most massages turn into sex. You can be the aggressor, grip her by the throat, whisper some nasty freaky shit in her ear, throw her on the bed then eat her pussy. If it does come to having a conversation, do not beg, make her feel bad for not giving you sex, or putting together a schedule to have sex; you don't want sex to feel like a job. Just explain your needs; ask for her needs as well.

One day six months down the line since the video posting, I returned home from the second job as an evening janitor. I sat on the ugly green sofa in the living room to get a third wind to make late-night dinner. This is when Twitter was at its peak; everybody and their mothers were on this addicting app in 2009. At the time, I was scrolling reading tweets I received a random text message from a 501-area code.

"Hey, my name is Danni I'm 41 years old and have been married to Debra for three years. I'm worried and desperate for assistance. My wife complains daily that I'm not satisfying her sexually anymore. I discovered your video on YouTube. I performed a trick I'd seen on the video and Debra went insane. Please I need your help. I'll pay whatever."

These weren't the exact word in the text, I kind of exaggerated the "I need help" line for a fact, he seemed hollow inside and surely desperate. Especially for reaching out to a 24-year-old black man who was basically bullshitting on camera. I did not reply to his text until the next day, I had to unwind from the two jobs that drained me day-to-day.

The next morning, I replied attempting to write in a professional matter. This was before I became a writer. I did not have a clue on how to put words in a sentence to sound executive. "Thanks for reaching out to me, I can definitely get you two on the right track. I have a few questions before we start this program. How is your relationship outside of the bedroom? when was the last time you two went on an actual date?" The mental, respect, and love have to be balanced to have great sex when it's marriage or a long-term relationship. Do you do foreplay, roleplay, have spontaneous intimate moments, light candles, and set the mood with relaxing music? What does she complain about the most?"

Danni responded two days following the message I sent. I thought he chickened out in view that I actually acknowledged his message. He explained that his wife and himself were maintaining a healthy mental relationship outside the bedroom, he mentioned that she's mostly sexually frustrated with him, she's not turned on, he also said "When I do attempt to foreplay or roleplay it seems forced and she complains about that too." I replied to Danni's message this time with a price and package, this was my first time actually coaching a couple so I was not definite about the payment. I googled top paying sex therapists; they made approximately $306,000 a year. I divided the $306,000 by 12 which broke down to $24,000 a month then divided the four weeks in a month which came down to $6,000 a week. That's when I settled with $1,000 to teach over the phone for a week since the couple lived in a different state or $1,900 two days; I'd actually observe and guide them through their sex session but they had to get a room and flight to Pittsburgh.

I honestly was considering lowering the price, in my mind I thought, "There is no way anyone would pay this." The same feeling Jen Sincero felt in her book, "you are a badass for making money." She held her breath when giving a quote for $6,000 for coaching. When I sent the text with the fee, all the air escaped my lungs. Within an hour I received a text "yes, that's perfect. I will do both packages. A week of preparation then the wife and I will come to PA for the last session."

I was caught by surprise. Even though I knew the amount that I was getting I still pulled the calculator app up and added them both together. It was in fact $2,900. Then out of nowhere, my anxiety shot through the roof. I began questioning myself, doubting myself, and even had thoughts of not teaching. Sometimes the inner self can block your blessings. It's not always the naysayers who will tell you what you shouldn't do. In that instant, I had the idea of purchasing a white gold chain and a hefty name charm that read "TINK" in diamonds. The mature me now of days, would invest that money in something else but soon as knew what I wanted the ideas flowed like water. The reason why I write notes and daily affirmation until this day is because when you manifest, have a positive mindset, or use words that will uplift you, you are most likely to succeed.

Although Danni said their marriage was healthy; I believed he was telling half of the truth, I can be inaccurate he could be truthful but I felt when a woman is sexually frustrated, she can be a bit evil, just like a hungry woman; she can become bitchy. He wired the $1000 to me and agreed to pay the rest at the beginning of the next class. When I spoke to Danni for the first time, he sounded like a Hillbilly cowboy on a black and white Midwest movie. The guy was super country. I imagine him with a ten-gallon hat, chewing

Tabaco with tight Wrangler Pants and dirty cowboy boots with spurs on the back.

Each morning we spoke I provided him with a task.

1.) Cook or order take out or have a candlelight dinner. Have conversations other than work or the negative that's happening around. Talk about the past, how you felt when you met one other, your childhood, or places you would like to travel. Keep the conversation interesting by getting to know each other once again. Laugh about the goofy shit you've done. Sometimes good exchanges of words can be better than sex. Watch a good movie, play games entertain her the best you can to have her glowing.

2.) Depending on the woman, some are exceedingly insecure regarding their bodies. There's are women with heavy bodies, slim figures, thick shapes, and fit; in my eyes, all shapes can get it. I instructed him to massage his woman and touch all areas of the body firmly with oil. Compliment her body, make her feel like you adore every flaw she believes she has. Make her feel desirable, secure of her figure. This will build confidence mentally when it comes to her structure. In a long period of time of dating someone or marriage, a minority of men sometimes forget to praise their women from time to time. Another man's recognition may not add up to the man she loves. I also expressed that he should eat her pussy, last time he performed oral on Debra she was highly satisfied. Shot out to the YouTube video.

3.) Distance yourself, you don't want smoother her with too much attention all in one week. Find some time to work on yourself. Get a haircut, have drinks with your boys, visit a friend or family member, get lost in Home Depot or whatever store you desire. Pretend to be busy. Even though you two live in the same house, give her space and a chance to miss you. This works especially for men who are pursuing a woman; be consistently take her on dates, talk to her every day, buy gifts, show her different for a few weeks then fall back with the dry conversation, less time spent, and become unreachable. This is the hot and cold method which is hell of evil and fucked up. Make a woman fall for you by spoiling her with consistency, tender comfort, and a man's guidance, and then slightly disappear. This will have a woman's mind stranded with confusion, and missing the fuck out of you. Right, when you feel like she's falling off that's when you pursue some more. Not all women will fall for this as some are ten steps ahead of the game.

4.) I began the package on a Tuesday. On Thursday, Danni and I talked for an hour every day. 30 minutes in the morning and 30 during the evening. This time I had to prepare Danni for a sexual encounter with his wife therefore we spoke a little more than an hour in the morning. It was his big day. I told him to text her something sexual that she takes pleasure in. Since he became advanced at tongue painting. I voiced "You should say some simple shit like; Tonight, I want your pussy on my face until you cum." If she responds in a positive manner give her a visual in words on how you would perform devouring her box. The thought of herself grinding against your face will be a seed planted in her mind depending on the day she's having. Tonight, make sure she's completely naked, blindfold Debra with a scarf, bandanna, or whatever you have to cover her eyes. Once one of the five senses are absent the others will become stronger; your touch will become more effective and you'll have her speculating your next move unless she's peeking. Have Debra lay on her stomach then slowly drop warm or room temperature oil on her back; like day two give your woman a firm massage. This time in the midst of caressing with your hands; plant soft kisses on her neck, collar, and random destinations on the back. Be at ease, don't overthink, and feel the vibration of her soul. Massage her ass with a stern grasp; palm both cheeks and rub them as well. Each word I uttered Danni's response was "un hum, um hum." He was listening closely and repeating each sentence gradually as if he was taking notes.

"Palm. Both. Cheeks. And. Rub. Them." He said calmly.

"Inch your thumbs down to the vagina, spit the outer lips (labia minor) apart then massage them by opening and closing the lips. Depending on how moist she is, the pussy will make a smacking noise each time you open her up. You have a ton of options; you can eat her from the back, have her perched on both knees, and like an auto mechanic you can slide on your back beneath her then guide your lady to take a seat on your face or you can flip her around on the back and eat her in the regular missionary position. Whatever position you decide to snack; ensure that it's easy to access to plug yourself in her. When you thrust; operate your waist and not your back. (Lamara Teaching I expressed) Since this will be a relaxing environment; gradually slide your manhood inside, you don't have to jam your dick in her. Send a small number of short strokes then feed your woman all inches of yourself, sink down to the bottom; all in moderation. Once you feel that she has a feel for you, pick up the tempo. Listen to the breathing, pay attention to the hand motion, moans, and the rhythm and swaying of her body. I myself listen to the rhythmical pattern when penetrating, depending on how wet the box is; you'll hear a drenching noise each time you bury it. When the intensity builds up don't be afraid to grasp her neck, smack her ass, grasp her ankles or talk dirt. There are no rules in the bedroom." There's a lot more I coached nevertheless you have to continue reading to attain deeper.

006. Class in Session

"How it go?" I asked with excitement rolling off my tongue. He huffed, blowing frustration through the airwave. "We didn't do nothing last night." He said as if he was at a close friend's funeral; he sounded miserable.

"Why? What happened?" my excitement drowned in a pool of sympathy.

"She stopped at my mother-in-law's house for a few hours after work, then came home with a serious attitude. She was exhausted by the time she walked through the door. I did tell her we're visiting Pittsburgh for an erotic coaching. She was interested and asked plenty of questions."

The Married couple flew 900 miles from Little Rock to Pittsburgh and got a five-star hotel downtown. Before I actually met the two I went grocery shopping; I bought blueberries, raspberries, blackberries, strawberries, dark chocolate then ran to the liquor store and bought two bottles of red wine. In one of the magazines, I read that berries enhance the sex drive; the anti-oxidants will increase blood flow to the sex organs. These foods will also intensify the sexual stimulation and give you two an arousing thrill during lovemaking. The red wine will also increase the blood flow, plus will have you open up after two or three glasses. Red wine will sneak up on you like a haunted house employee dressed in a scary costume. The first time I drank red wine with a woman sex followed. We literally fucked for hours, the sexual frequency was high. It seemed like we were attempting to fuck each other souls out of the flesh. Then again she was a Leo woman, all my experiences with the lion women were beyond mind-blowing. I drank wine with a

Virgo woman and it was the same mind-blowing result. Until this day in my 30's if you ask any woman that visits they'll probably tell you I offered them red wine.

In the hotel lobby, I was approached by a tall lengthy, white guy dressed in a navy-blue button-up shirt, his sleeves were rolled to the forearms, he had khaki pants on, and wore some royal blue and white running shoes. It was Danni. He reached for an embrace.

"Nice to finally meet you." His handshake was firm and his accent was country but definitely not the cowboy I pictured the first time I spoke to him on the phone.

"Nice to me you as well. How was the flight?" I asked

"Long, but I slept almost the entire way here."
"How long? three to four hours?" I wasn't sure.
"Yes, four hours. We got here around 12 pm."
"Damn, that's a long time sitting on the plane. Question."
"Yes. What's up?" he said walking towards the elevator, reaching in his pocket; I followed beside him.

"Does Debra have any clues on what's about to happen?"
"Sort of, she been asking a lot of questions about the coaching since I told her we were coming here." He pulled out a handful of cash and a key card for the elevator.

"I sure hope she'll be comfortable with me being here," I said as I watched Danni press the up button to the elevator.

"We'll have to see, man. This is something new to us." He uttered as the red number over top of the elevator count down from 5 to 4

"What's in the bag?" He continued.

"I bought some fruit and wine to show my appreciation," I said as the elevator dinged and the door spilled open in the time the number struck one. When we stepped in between the open doors, he handed over a stack of money.

"Let me give you this before I forget."

7th floor; room 704 a right off the elevator Danni slid the card in the door, and the lock automatically clicked. Following behind Danni I entered the room. A heavy-set, biracial woman with short curly hair, in her mid 30's or early 40's dressed in Jeans and a salmon pink shirt sat her phone down and stood up from the farther bed next to the window. I was actually surprised at her appearance. Danni the country white boy had himself a sister and she was actually very attractive.

"This is my wife Debra. This is coach Tink." Danni introduced us. When we grasped one another's hands to shake this is when my anxiety struck again. I felt like shrinking into the thin carpet of the hotel floor right in front of the married couple. Behind this inviting, trustworthy face my heart was thumping rapidly as I spoke to my conscious

"Just breath slow, you got this."

"Nice to meet you, I heard so much about you."

Fifteen minutes after the meet and greet I had Danni and Debra sit on the bed beside the window. Before we all became settled I explain the reasons for the berries, chocolate, and wine. I myself poured a tall glass to rattle the nervousness out of my system plus to be the teacher my confidence had to be on a high frequency. I sat on the bed closest to the door with my second glass of wine in hand, as I spoke facing the two.

"Okay, with this session I will need for you two to be fully open with each other and understanding. This class is strictly about sex, nothing else more. I'm not a relationship therapist. Also, Debra are you comfortable with me being in the room watching you two have sex?" Her eyes shifted side to side, her head slightly jerked back as her eyes squint low; the black side of her roots surfaced for a split second as she sluggishly glanced at Danni.

"You did not say nothing about us having sex in front of this man."

Danni looked nervous as he replied as his words tripped over his tongue. "You, you been, been complaining so I asked. I had to seek help to better our sex. His videos on YouTube is the reason why you love when I eat your pussy darling. Please just this one time."

Debra turned her attention to me. "So basically, you're going to guide him."

"Yes, not just him. The both of you. This is a two-way session."

"Okay, this is unexpected. I wish I would've known the exact details I would've dressed casually.

"It's fine, I'm not judgmental," I said sipping the wine. I turned all lights off except the dim desk light in the corner then sat back in place. "Debra."

"Yes." She answered.

"Sexually, what frustrates you the most?" I asked.

"I'm not satisfied, there's no passion it feels like I'm having sex with someone who doesn't care. He cums in minutes and when he's done, most of the time he rolls over then sleeps. I haven't came from penetration in over a year. I finally able to cum from oral sex in the last couple weeks." "What's the difference between the past and now? There had to be some type of sexual connection before marriage? I asked

"There was a connection at the beginning, he was able to last longer, he seemed to be more into pleasing me. He doesn't institute or try to have sex with me. He barely kisses me. I don't remember the last time I felt his tongue in my mouth. Truth be told I'm bored." Debra said candidly laying down her emotions on the table. Danni's face became red as an electric stove on high; he had a look that displayed he was craving to speak to defend himself; before he could say his truths I asked him the same question that I asked Debra.

"So Danni, Sexually, what frustrates you the most?"

"She complains about each and everything. It gets to a point that I don't want to have sex because I can predict what the outcome will be. To me, the sex is as pleasing as it was years ago. I don't understand what the problem is but I'm doing my absolute best."

"Let's make this clear I'm neutral. I listened to both sides." I said before stating my opinion." I paused staring between the two of them. "I'm going to start with Danni, what it sounds like, Debra wants more intimacy out of you; she also wants you to focus more on her requirements rather than rolling over when you get a nut. As an alternative, if you do happen to cum before her; duck low, put your face between her thighs then flick your tongue across that kitty to finish." I said in a teacher's voice. "Now you Debra, instead of bashing him. You can teach him. Tell him what you enjoy, if you want to experience some new sex ideas share them with him. Tell him to be aggressive. Be exact in what you want, if not on no occasion he will know." I told them the story about the New Orleans woman Lamara teaching me and how she was vocal about what she yearned for.

"Danni, look your wife in the eyes." He showed signs of uneasiness.
He turned his attention away from me then glanced at his woman with hesitation

"Like this?" He asked

"Yes, pretend that I'm not here. Listen and focus on each other." I said in a calming tone. "Close your eyes then head in for a kiss." In unison, they shut their eyes and leaned forward to bond lips. The peck turned into intimate tongue tangling.
Tongue kissing for women who take delight in slithering the love language, sent a wave of chills through their body, which signals to the pussy, to create a water flow like no other. I had plenty of women cum from tongue wrestling, no penetration, no eating the box or caressing anywhere near the vagina. For myself, deep kissing gave me a tingle in my balls and toes. It's the weirdest feeling. Speaking of a weird feeling as I sat there observing; I felt like a creep, out of place and a bit uncomfortable but the ball of money lumped inside of my pocket reminded me to remain composed.

"Don't be afraid to touch each other," I said, sipping down the last of the wine.

"Grab the back of her neck, explore deeper in her mouth." Danni followed my instruction; Within seconds

Debra's moans were bouncing off the hotel walls; she was genuinely connected and into the moment. "So, I want you to continue on; I'll interrupt if needed. Again, pretend I'm not here." I said to the both of them, then I kept speaking this time to Danni "You can do a little foreplay, slightly graze your teeth or slide your tongue across her neck and collar. Grasp her neck firmly; take control."

The couple proceeded, Danni grabbed Debra by the throat and continued to slob her down, he then clinched onto her jaw to lift her head back to fully exposed her neck. Debra's eyes were shut tight and her mouth was wide open as he glided his tongue against her neck; he glazed his saliva all over from earlobe to earlobe.

"Begin to remove clothes, start by taking off the top but keep the fire blazing." Swiftly Danni lifted Debra's shirt off then removed his.

"Now Debra kiss on his chest." The couple seemed to become comfortable as the session went on. Danni laid back in the middle of the bed in the time Debra seductively brushed her hands up his hairy chest as she gazed down into his eyes. She leaned towards his body then landed smooches on his collar, then gradually down his chest to his stomach. While I sat on the edge of the bed across I critiqued every move. Debra was on fire, she had the glare of a sex demon. In my thoughts as Deb loosened his pant, I knew she was going in for the kill when she began kissing and licking around his belly button. She yanked his pants down along with his Hanes Boxers; pulling them halfway down his thighs. Debra turned out to be freakier than I thought she would be. At first, she seemed innocent but those be the ones. Soon as his manhood fell out she covered her mouth over top then started to suck in a fast motion. I considered telling her to take her time blowing as she blew him down but Danni seem to enjoy the speedy head so on second thought I kept my mouth closed. We men have different preferences when to comes to getting head; some of us are like Danni who rather get rapid neck when the head bounces up and down in haste like a paddle ball on a string. Then you have the men who take pleasure when a woman takes her good ole time caressing the dick with their mouth, licking around the cone while stroking, cascading the tongue down the length then slowly sliding it up, spit bubbles, soaking hands, tongue slapping and etc. Debra kept the momentum flowing, her hand jerked Danni's knob while she continued to throw her face on him.

"Take control, place your hand on her head," I said watching Danni position his hand on her head gently as if he was petting a cat.

"Moan while you suck his dick, talk to him and slurp too. Make love to that shit." I gassed Debra; she was sucking with no emotions. The sound of a woman slurping, moaning, and sometimes talking to the dick will mentally have a man overly aroused; especially if the head is messy. Being the dominator and seeing his woman being dominated can be the biggest turn-on for a man during intercourse. Debra spat on his manhood, a string of saliva stretched three to four inches from his penis to the tip of her tongue; she gazed in his eyes with erotic flares in her pupils then drop her whole face down on him. She stroked his saturated dick as she sucked and dramatically slurped. Sounding like she was sucking the last bite of liquid through a straw in a smoothie. Danni's hands were now covering his face

"Oh yes baby, oh yes baby." He wailed in his Midwest accent.

"Cum for me, cum for me," Debra demanded with her tongue on display. Danni growled.

"Yes, yes, yes." Within a few seconds Danni glanced down, face redder than a fire extinguisher, growling louder as he shots over her tongue and lips. This is not what I wanted the outcome to be, but since Debra was so into giving him head; I decided to let her finish him.

"Your turn," I spoke to Danni. Debra was fully sensual; she was prepared and completely naked. Since Danni praised his oral abilities, I allowed him to perform without saying a peep. He did a slight bit of foreplay, kissed from her neck to biting on the inner thighs, firmly caressed her body while he ate the box, he kept his focus on stimulating the clit, and did everything I explained in the video. I suggested one thing while Danni ate her essence.

"Debra rub your foot against his dick." This was a secret move that I experienced; which I had major results in making women cum faster than usual. I'm not sure the reason why the outcome is so frequent. I think when a woman's foot slides on the man's hard wood while he's having her as a meal is an indication of hardness and what she has coming excited her mind. Debra's foot drifted upon his penis, shifting up and down against it. In the time, Danni carried on feasting. Her wailings grew noisier like I Danni was turning the volume up from her pussy.

"Keep going, keep going," I said in a low convincing tone, to inspire Danni.

"Breath out your nose, keep going." I continued as Debra's foot slipped off his dick. She grabbed the head with both hands pushing his face in. Danni's tongue whipped side to side beating the clit steadily. Both of her feet were rooted deep in the mattress as she lifted her waist upward and pushed harder down on Danni's head.

"Fuck, fuck, fuck I'm cumming." She expressed as she climaxed over his chin. Debra looked decompressed as she

glared down at Danni with a slightly satisfying grin on her
face.

"Did you enjoy that?" I asked.

"Yes I did, absolutely." She said.

"By your motions and moans, I can tell. And Danni
you did an amazing job. I didn't have to say too much."

"Thank you, I did my best."

"You surprised the hell out of me man. So, are
you'll ready for the second lesson."

"Yes." They said in a tiny bit of unison. They were
all in now. There wasn't a nervous soul in this room;
including myself.

"Now ease your dick in her." Since she was beyond
wet caused by his saliva and her own natural juices, plugging
himself in shouldn't have been a challenge, the outer and
inside should've been slippery. Danni leaned forward chest
to chest, waist between Debra's open thighs with his right
hand guiding himself unhurriedly into the vagina. Debra let a
modest moan slip out between her lips as he inserted himself
inch by inch until there were no inches to engulf. He began
to stroke at a slow pace for the first half of a minute then he
lifted himself up; distancing from her chest, attempting to
shift to impatience pace. This is when I noticed the sway of
his stroke terribly changed; he was now using his whole
entire body to penetrate. The separated problem, he
immediately never gave Debra a chance to feel his full
affection. While he thrust his way in full steam for the half of
minute I observed, I assumed Debra wasn't enjoying the
moment, the way she reacted to the oral sex was completely
different than how she reacted to getting dicked down. In the
midst of thrusting in full steam, I interrupted Danni.

"Hey! Hey! Hey! Stop for one minute." I said abruptly. He paused in mid-stroke and glared at me as his chest heaved in and out. Debra gazed my way as well, looking like a dead fish with a dick inside of her.

"Man, remember what we talked about? You have to take your time. Get acquainted with the rhythm of her body, you have to match her energy."

"Okay. so, I need to slow down?" He questioned.

"Yes, sway your hips when you're stroking." I grasped the nearest pillow, did a brief demonstration on the soft cushion that supported our necks at night. I posted the pillow in front of me then rocked my waist into the rectangular bag.

"Sway your hips like this." I humped the pillow one more again. Until this day when I think about this moment of grinding against a fucking pillow and I cringe. What in the hell was I thinking?

"Debra, you have to be vocal. Tell him his mistakes or what he's doing right. Communication is the key to amazing sex." I continued "Danni eat her pussy again." Danni went down for a short time to get Debra halfway aroused.

"Let's try this again." He climbed over top of his woman, plugging himself inside in a missionary position; chest to chest.

"Now kiss her and slowly sway them hips."

"Give me your tongue. you got this baby" Debra said. Not even a second later their tongues were twisting and turning in all types of ways. Danni gradually swung his mid-section between her thighs.

"Push deep inside. At that same pace." I uttered. He took my advice; driving deep as he can reach.

"Fuck him back, Debra. when you feel, him coming down bring yourself up." They were off rhythm for a split second until Debra grasped hold of his butt to get him in sequence. Personally, I don't like my butt grabbed but for Danni to get with the flow I understood. Once they were fully synced, the sexual energy shifted electrifyingly. The "oh yes, yes, the oh My god, the right there." Escaped out Debra's mouth. Danni moaned and groaned.

Finally, they were on the same frequency as one other. Positions alternated from doggy style at a mild pace and I made him push down on the back to create an arch as he grabbed hold of her neck. When she rode his manhood, I had Danni firmly rub his hands all over her back. I told him to plant his feet in the mattress for leverage to push upwardly as she slid down him. The grand finale happened when I instructed Danni to lift his woman's legs over his shoulders in the time her lower back hang halfway on the side of the bed, as he stood strong on foot to penetrate while he pulled her in by the thighs. Each stroke he delivered in a mild pace Debra went completely insane, her hands cuffed the sheets tightly as moans spilled out like a tipped glass of water. Not to be disrespectful but her juice box was singing; it was making the noises that sounded like stirred yogurt with a spoon as he shifted in and out. Danni was weak in the knees, glaring at the ceiling. His stroke dwindled slowly; without a doubt, I knew he was on the verge of finishing.

"Oh fuck!" he wailed "oh fuck!" He said pulling his manhood out and roaring as he shot clear liquid on her stomach.

"Hurry and eat the pussy." I said pacing back and forth; immediately he dropped to his knees. A woman is highly sensitive after she's been stimulated by penetration which makes it 10 times easier for her climax or for some women it's too much to take. One lick to the clit is like lighting a fire to a wick that's connected to a bomb. Danni swept his tongue against her love button; within a minute Debra's soul lifted from the hotel bed. I leaned on the wooden desk with a humongous smile stretching across my face. Danni stood up butt naked with socks on, swiftly I threw a towel at his chest, and then I tossed a towel on the bed next to Debra. Debra was too delicate to move so Danni volunteer to cover her limp body.

"I haven't felt this way in so long." She said, speaking in a drained low tone. Danni sat on the foot end of the bed and grinned as if her word was like music to his ears.

"Thanks, man, I appreciate you. This was an experience of a lifetime."

"I'm so glad I can help." We spoke about the moment they enjoyed.

The second day was the same session but I allowed them to fuck without me saying as much as the day before. I spoke to the couple twice or sometimes three times a year since then. They were in a good healthy place in their relationship since I spoke to them eight years ago, before I switched from Android to iPhone and lost all contacts, including changing my phone number. I wished Danni and Debra the best. Thereafter them I coached eight more clients.

007. Relationship Status

In my duration of life, I experienced a variety of relationships. *General love*; the love you thought will never end. *The lustful relation*; the addiction of sex collaborative that feels like never-ending love but in reality, without the great intercourse they're two empty souls. *Forceful devotion*; the relationship you thought will put you in a better position. so, you decide to be with this person because it only makes sense but at the same time, you're not really into them, even if they grow on you as the months pass, your conscience still tells you differently. *The toxic affiliation*; the hot and cold relationship where you two are in harmony with each other then the next minute attempting to rip one another neck's off. Most people can't get away from this shit. The worst for any man is being pussy whipped; the pussy-whipped man is the most fragile, the woman can lie, cheat, spend all his funds and disrespect him. This is the man who will stick around faithfully. It happens to the best of us. Your nose would be so wide open a bird can fly inside. Women same for you, I'm sure plenty of you'll be dickmotized. Where a man treated you like a smashed ketchup package under a shoe and you still took him back because of the feeling of how great he fucked you. Last but least *The One*; the one is that one person who has been around for years, you can call them any time after your breakup, during your separation until you and the significant other eventually get on good terms. They're the person you can visualize yourself with, had a few attempts of being in a relationship but no matter what it's never successful; but they're around when needed. I'm going to explain each one of these types of relationships briefly in a short story. This book is to show growth in me, not to expose or to hurt anyone; so, I will change names, locations, and useful pieces of information to hide the identity of the women in these stories. Like I said at the opening of the book. "I was lethal to some women and a blessing to others. I honestly can admit I wasn't always in the right."

Forced Devotion

2013 New Year's Day: It was past 12am so technically it was the first day of the year. After the club in the Strip District, I swung past a house party held in East Liberty hosted by Chester known as Chestnut, and his older sister Tiffany also known as Tiff Wee-Wee. Both of them were funny individuals and hometown comedians. They were also part of the East Liberty Originals, the OG's of East Liberty and so was I. At this party, I stumbled across this brown round-face woman I met six years earlier at a club where there was nothing but a handful of Blacks surround by white people 18 and up. A Black person in this club was effortless to spot; you could literately count on one hand the blacks in the building. She was the first Black woman I spotted from the opposite side of the club. I was in good company and drinking with my younger brother Devon. I mentioned to Devon that I had to get at this woman in the little black dress. There probably were 100 different women with black dresses on but Devon knew which one I was talking about.

"You talking about the girl over there?" He nodded pointing with his head, not to draw any attention.

"Yes her. Watch, I'm about to swerve yo." I said with a great bit of confidence as I took a sip of the liquid courage. After a few swigs, I placed the drink on the small circular table.

"Watch this." I stood up then began my journey towards the girl. I had to admit because Devon my baby brother and this was our first time in a club together I had to eat every word I said and demonstrate that his brother was the M.A.N. So, I strolled through the dancing crowd, the beaming colorful strobe lights darted each and every direction as the techno music boomed. I felt my brother's eyes glued on my back in the location I left him. He was observing my every step, probably taking mental notes. I also noticed the woman whom I had my eyes on gazed at me. I shot her a smile as she came closer and closer; dodging the aggressive techno dancers. After the walk that felt like a mile, I approached.

"I know you from somewhere?" these were the only words that cumulated in my mind. One of the lamest pickup lines that is still used today by men all across the world. At this moment, this line picked up because she replied nicely

"I know, I was thinking the same thing." We exchanged words for no longer than five minutes. In the short conversation, we figured out we didn't know one other. Patrice was her name; she voiced the basics that are spilled when meeting someone for the first time. We exchanged age, zodiac sign, and where she resided. We exchanged numbers then met the week after. I'm not going to put in detail what happened, just say we were being grown on the couch on a late-night mission. After this night, we were literally sexually partners. She lived an hour away from Pittsburgh. So, Once or twice a month I would take that dreaded drive to the far suburban to sleep with Patrice. On the plus side; Patrice was a clubber; she would be in the city almost every weekend. Many nights she came over to my place after the club or we would randomly cross paths with each other in the clubs. Nine times out of ten when she was in the city, we were intimate.

Fast forward to the New year's party six years later, we were both under the influence of alcohol in the same scene. Two months before New Year's Day; Hard times crept on me unexpectedly. Instead of paying my rent, I decided to pay the $1,600 to get my vehicle repaired then soon after that I was terminated from the primary paying job. With my money spent and no money flowing in, I was forced to move back to my Parents' house. Now as I'm writing this my decision to pay for car repair rather than a roof over my head was the dumbest decision. We both had desires for one other and it had been over a year since we slept together. I basically was homeless. Any man over 25 living with his parents is homeless. So, we had no choice but to take the risk to drive an hour to her place. Surly the alcohol level was past the PA State requirements. I followed her home, the entire drive to the destination it was as if I had weights over my eyelids. Even worse while she drove, the sky seemed like it was closing in on me. Soon as we stepped in the house and come out from the brutal January weather we were ripping clothes off which led to a night of sexual activities.

Three months later

"I'm pregnant."
"It's not mine," was my bitchass response.

Five months in, she tweeted the gender. She also tweeted the name she had in mind for the child. The name did not fit with me, not one bit. Later that night sitting in front of the computer in the process of finishing the first book I called Patrice. I apologized for my ignorance and agreed to step up, she suggested that I move out of my mother's and come live with her. I didn't accept or deny her offer. Instead, I stayed over once and twice a week. Every time I spent the night she would cook a fire-ass dinner. If a woman has a cabinet full of seasonings other than your everyday salt, pepper & Lawry's seasoned salt; she can cook guaranteed. Patrice was stuffing me like a build a bear. Two days a week increased to four, four increased into an entire month a month turned into every day. I blamed her cooking. I was literally stuck. When they say, good food is the key to a man's heart that quote is true in all cases. I promised on my soul just because she is one of my child mothers that when I sell more than a million copies of this book, my goal will be to give her a restaurant or bakery no matter how much she despises me.

Within months, I was gaining massive weight by the end of the relationship I was 45 pounds more than I was entering in.

During our relationship, I couldn't stop dealing with women; I honestly didn't want to be in the relationship. I continued because she was pregnant and this time around, I did not want my child to not have a father in the home. I habitually lied about my whereabouts so much that I felt as if I was telling the truth. I remember this one night my homeboy Chip, his parents were out of town. Chip's people lived in a humongous house in the eastern suburbs of Pittsburgh. Wade, Chip, and I invited a house full of women. When I say, this night was epic I'm not exaggerating. Girls were walking around naked, girls in the Jacuzzi, girls dancing on the pole, licking on each other and of course we had sex with them in different rooms.

I gave Patrice a courtesy call in the upstairs bathroom where it was mostly quiet. I lied saying that my car broke down; I also told her that I wouldn't be able to come home. Right after we spoke I turned my phone off then enjoyed the rest of the night. A long time ago before my father became a saved man he gave me pointers on getting out of cheating. One was never to break daylight, long as you get in the house before the sun comes up; possibly you'll be in the safe place. Another was a story about how he didn't come home to his girlfriend at the time. He opened the hood of the car, brushed his hand over the engine then paint his shirt with the oily grim to show evidence. I did just that and mostly his logic worked. I had a side woman who bought me a second phone; a sky blue iPhone four. She's the reason why I prefer iPhone until this day. My side woman gave me all the head I desired. When I was at home Patrice seldom gave me oral. The iPhone was the hidden-phone Patrice didn't know about. I gave this number to all my new and old shorties. With all the lies and cheating the household became depressing.

Months after our child was born I started an effort to be a faithful man toward this woman. Mentally I think she was done with our relationship months before we completely broke up. When I punched the clock after two jobs, I still managed to come home in good spirits. All happy and full of joy, kissing her kids and my new child as well. Patrice would give me an unconvincing kiss and scroll through the phone without saying too much. No matter how she was feeling inside; she still cooked dinner every day. It was like the dark cloud was our ceilings. On social media, we looked to be the most heartwarming couple with the photogenic photos with the amusing caption. Between those four walls, we couldn't stand one other but we gambled for our little one. As time went on we argued, we never came to an agreement, I said some bitch ass shit that I will mention later in the book. There was this Black cat that would cross me once in a while when I parked my car. Lie to you not. Every time I set eyes on the midnight black furball, something extremely bad would happen between Patrice and me. This one time after seeing the cat sprint under the dumpster in all fours, Patrice found my blue iPhone while I was in the shower. When I got out of the shower, the bedroom door was locked. I heard her talking to the side woman through the wooden doors on the speakerphone. The side woman was running down every bit of information from the time we shared to the time we slept together, down to the days I went to her house. After this day, Patrice was exceedingly damaged.

This is when the roles shifted. When a man fucks up to a great degree his insecurities began to seep out like grease in a sponge. Patrice started to step out more frequently while I or her parents watched our child. She began to come home later than usual. When she went on a trip to Vegas with a group of women and men from Pittsburgh she answered the phone once out of the four days she was on vacation. One of the most uncomfortable moments in my life was when she came home from Vegas I picked her up from the International Airport along with the friends she was with. Soon as Patrice sat down in the passenger's seat with her phone in hand, a text with the man's name and a text that read, "Did you make it home yet?" displayed on the screen. In a bitch ass way, I confronted Patrice in front of her friends.

"Oh that's why you didn't answer your phone, you probably were fucking some ni**a." Surely, to the friends, I was every part of a bitch. Now of days I would never. After I saw that text I was searching through her phone daily like Dora the Explorer. Another bitch ass trait. Man, or woman I don't care what sex you are if you feel the need to explore through someone phone to find signs of cheating. Clearly, you shouldn't be with this person. It's a waste of energy and it's soul-draining. Then when you don't find nothing you'll feel dumb as shit deep inside. Remember everything that's done in the dark will come to the light. This one day at the end of September, Patrice and I got into a fuming altercation. I'm not definite what the argument was about but the dark cloud over us was pouring. Tables were flipped on the floor, hurtful words were exchanged, my laptop along with my car keys was thrown in the dumpster outside, pushing and shoving was involved, the animosity for one other filled atmosphere. This devilish night compelled us to separate for the entire month of October.

During month eleven, thirteen days in, I met a character whom you'll read about in a chapter in the future. The character I met on the 13th, we had a swift togetherness for the remainder of the month and half of November until she abruptly cut me off over a conversation on the phone. In the trail of getting flung down, I sweet-talked myself into Patrice's good grace. We shared a peaceful Thanksgiving and

Christmas together as a family then when New Year's circled the block this was when my karma came to strike.

New Year's Eve 2014 Patrice and I agreed that we were going to celebrate New Year's this year with our friends. Earlier in the day, I noticed that she shaved her box clean and the last time she shaved was in the summer when she wore a bikini on our family vacation. Since then not a razor or wax, or even an eye of attention was given to her grooming habits. Some women get waxed and steam cleaned regularly then some get it on special occasions and then some didn't believe in removing their natural hairs. To be honest, it didn't matter to me just keep it clean. My conscience was screaming intuition that afternoon; I knew for a fact something was bound to happen.

11:58 PM two minutes before the ball dropped Patrice FaceTimed me and at the time I was in the crowded club. I answered

"Hey, babe I just want to make sure you're not kissing any girls for New Year's." She voiced,

"I'm not," I confirmed, even though I was entertaining every woman that crossed my path that night. The countdown began as we remained on the phone 10.9.8.7.6.5.4.3.2.1 everyone in the club in unison hooted "HAPPY NEW YEAR'S" Patrice and I exchanged our happy New Year's. Then before hanging up she said

"I Love You. Babe." Now this "I love you" she uttered just didn't feel authentic, it was odd and random. This "I love you." Felt like there was guilt behind the three words. Someone can tell you "I love you" a million times to the face, if there isn't loyalty standing next to the three words that expression is irrelevant.

In the time following the club, I went to an after-hour, hole-in-the-wall strip club in McKees Rocks, Pa. I watched dancers slide down the pole for approximately an hour and had a choice to ride home to my family or follow this beautiful woman who was dying to throw me some pussy. It was 3 am on New Year's morning, and it would've been nice to wake up to my new child who was one at the time. So, I decided to ride home. When I pulled up to the complex I recognized there were different vehicles in the parking lot and a fancy car parked in the spot I'd parked in every day. When I parked, I remembered blowing fog into the cold January chill.

"Fuck" I said as I shut the door; feeling the bitter winter breeze spike through my skeleton. Soon as I went to take my first step guess what I saw? Yes, you guessed right. The black cat, this time the cat didn't run underneath the dumpster. It stood still as a statue, gazing at me as I made my way to the apartment. In my mind now since I identified the cat I expected some bull shit to happen. Patrice never locked the doors, either of us barely had a key for the place so as long as I lived in the apartment I'd just walk in. This particular night the front door was locked, I suspiciously hurried to the back door to check the entry. The back door was locked as well. As I remembered for months and months through the fall and winter, Patrice asked me to take the air conditioner out the window, and for those months, I procrastinated. Of course, this was in my lazy selfish days, when mindset to me didn't exist. The curtains were closed in the living room but there was a crack big enough for me to peep the scene. My child was sleeping on the floor, not on the couch but on the floor with no covers. It was cold, I had to make a decision to pull the A/C out of the window to climb through or drive an hour to my mother's house. I knew for a fact that the woman I could've gone home with was sleep or with another guy. Without a doubt, I slid the window up, grabbed a hold of the heavy A/C then sat it on the ground outside. I crawled through the window like a thief in the night; I rapidly slid the window down then picked him up off the floor and placed my child on the couch.

In one stride, I went through the kitchen, into the laundry room for something to cover his body. Everything considering this day seemed out of place. I thought about the shaved box, the strange "I love you.", the cars in the parking lot, the cat standing still, the locked doors, and my child sleeping not only alone but on the floor. I admitted climbing through the window was a terrible decision despite that my suspicions were tall.

Tiptoeing, step by step up the cracking wooden stairs I crept to the top. The lights shined through the cracks of the ajar bathroom door, providing me with enough light to see. The childrens' room door was opened and the master bedroom was closed. Right away I reached for the knob to find out the door was locked. Without thought I opened the bathroom door for an increase of light; right when I opened the door a bobby pin was at my toes screaming for me to grab hold of the thin bending metal. I restructured the bobby pin into a point and then stuck the object into the tiny hole in the middle of the doorknob. The lock popped, I twisted the knob, with awareness I opened the door and seen everything that played as a preview in my mind. I was dumbfounded. When I flicked the light on I detected men's jeans, Jordan shoes in conjunction with open condom wrappers, and some of her clothes. Four feet hung out the covers, the guy held Patrice close while they both slept peacefully like twin newborn babies; although the light shined above them. I stood there for a good 15 seconds digesting the scene in front of my eyes in disbelief. For some reason, I wasn't even upset. This was the end of a new beginning. This was what I needed to happen to break free. I grasped her ankle and then shook her leg. She didn't wake up. I wiggled their ankles again and got the same results but this time the heavy-set man woke up.

His eyes were wide like he saw a headlight of a truck coming head-on. When Patrice felt him move she woke up as well.

"What are you doing here." She said, playing dumb.

I do not blame the guy one bit, if a man was standing in front of me in an unfamiliar place my heart probably would jump out of my chest. I couldn't be mad at this man. He received what she was willing to give and going to jail for some pussy that's a no-no. I don't understand men who kill over one pussy then end up in prison with no pussy because that just doesn't add up. Then when the man is locked up nine out of ten, she'll be sleeping with another man.

I reached for the man's hand in a friendly gesture ignoring Patrice's question.
"Thanks for fucking my B***h, she's all yours," I said shaking his hand. He went along with it and responded.

"You're welcome."

That hour ride to my mother's house felt like ten hours. Truth be told I was bothered but at the same time, everything that played out was supposed to happen. I'll end this chapter by saying, never force yourself into something your heart isn't into. At the end of the day, someone will end up being hurt and it's a waste of time. I believed I got what I deserved. Anybody is replaceable.

008. The Lustful Relation

In 2015 at the beginning of February No Chill Radio, a podcast hosted by Yalocalbigghomie, Benji, Tiff-Wee-wee, and DJ Girl Quit Playing we had a wine night at a lounge in the strip district that was every Wednesday. Yolocalbigghomie invited me to be a special guest for the night. The place was a grown and sexy environment with a good mix of 90's popular hip-hop, R&B, and modern-day music. Young adults were vibing, socializing, blowing hookah smoke, and drinking all varieties of tasty wine under the pink dim lights. As a special guest, they gave me a complimentary bottle of wine. At the time, I was mounted at the bar alone as the bartender scrambled around to receive the wine I requested, I spotted a woman that I had been crushing on for a while on Instagram. I could say I was attracted to her buttery sugar brown skin, the pearly white smile, and her exotic bedroom eyes. Her height was at hand 5'5; she was petite with a nice little booty and a whole lot of tities. What I was attracted to the most was her long natural curly fro she displayed from time to time; this woman had hair for days. Through social media, the content she posted was explicit. The morning quotes she posted like "Suck your man dick before work," or a meme with a woman blowing a man's shaft with a quote over the photo saying "He shouldn't have to ask," had me assuming she was free-spirited.

I'm not going to fabricate this story I tried to shoot my shot in her messages before and was ignored. I could imagine all the thirsty men that slid in her messages after reading a stimulating quote, and it didn't make it any better that she was a dazzling woman. I knew that for a fact I was one of the many trying to get her attention. If you're a male attempting to shoot your shot through social media messaging, it's best not to compliment a photo of them half-naked with a bikini, twerk videos, or nasty quote posting. These are the official thirst traps that most of us men fall in. It may appear amusing but a thousand other men are thinking the same exact thing and ready to press send to their "Hey Queen." message. If you are going to send a woman a message, come differently because they probably heard all the beautiful compliments in the world. Spark a conversation about anything other than their appearance. If that doesn't work, then homeboy she's not interested, leave her the fuck alone.

When the bartender finally handed me the bottle of wine I sat with the radio hostess in their private section for no longer than 20 minutes as I chatted and drank with the crew I watched the woman with the curly fro and her heavyset friend walk towards the direction of the bathroom. The bathroom was not in the same facility as the lounge. You had to stroll through a fancy long hallway to get to the restroom. In the hallway, most women spent a lot of their time taking photos in front of the humongous mirror that covered the majority of the wall. Some minutes later after I marked the two heading towards the hallway, like a creep I navigated my way and followed their footsteps. When I turned the corner, she was in front of the mirror taking selfies along with the friend beside her. I can't remember vividly how I approached this woman but I do remember talking to her for a good period. We talked so long that her friend disappeared back into the lounge as we continued. I remembered this same night holding her in front of the mirror, telling her to take a glance at us and saying "we complement each other well." I also promised that I would be her Valentine. The Love Holiday was barely a week away. Her name was Peanut; we exchanged numbers after a half-hour of conversation and then went our separate ways.

In between Valentine's Day we hardly texted, she was a one-word texter. I thought I had Peanut in the bag after the night we met but judging off our texting she seemed not too interested. Even though our texting was dry as lips with no grease I was still a man of my word. The day before Valentine's Day I treated Peanut to lunch before attending work at 3pm. The next day, which was the actual holiday; I drove through the slippery snow-packed roads just to deliver roses, teddy bears, and chocolate. A woman loves when a man does what he vows. Applying just enough pressure can have a woman surrendered. Peanut's guard was now down. The one-word conversation turned into us Face Timing and texting more frequently.

Our second date was another wine night on a Wednesday. A bottle of wine was $25 and between the both of us, we drank the bottle until it was cleaned out. Each glass of wine she absorbed the more she became talkative and touchy-feely in public. Taking Peanut home the cold night sky hovered under the orange streetlights. Driving with one hand on the steering wheel, I turned my attention back and forth to the streets to glaring at Peanut as she gave me a seductive stare down. At the same moment, she bit her bottom lip. A few traffic lights later, she was caressing the throbbing bulge in my jeans with her tiny hand.

"It's big." She voiced more than once. When the yellow light transformed to red on Penn Avenue and Highland Avenue, smack dead in the middle of the East Liberty she popped the seat belt, facing towards me she balled on her knees in the passenger's seat, loosened my pants then fully exposed my already hardened curvy tube. I adjusted my seat back slightly and yanked my boxer briefs down a bit just in case she gave saturating oral. In the act of the light turning green; I tapped the accelerator, Peanut drizzled saliva from the tip of the tongue onto the cone of my manhood. Next, she slapped my heaviness against her hanging tongue then gently stroked the length of me. Closed stores, hair salons, and restaurants on each curb, I was riding down Highland Avenue with Peanut's face cascading down and up in repeat on all inches of this blackness as her curly afro bounced. For some apparent reason the better the head is while I'm driving the more focused I was on the road.

"There's a car next to us," I said in a warning low tone as I held the brake at a red light with the right turn single-clicking. Briefly gazing at the young black driver beside us. I guessed her first reaction was not to get caught. In an instant, she attempted to lift her head from my crotch. I swiftly pushed her back down and If she would have popped her head up like a jack in the box, for sure she would've revealed herself. Soon as I turned she brought her face up then sat back in the passenger's side smiling. If I had my own apartment, we would've been en route to my place but unfortunately, I was still laying my head in my old bedroom at my parents' house after the breakup two months earlier with Patrice. Peanut and I sat outside her mother's house for almost about 15 minutes; conversing, touching, and kissing as the heat coming out the vent kept us toasty.

"You want to come in?" she asked.

"Yes, are you sure? Are you sure you want me to meet your raise (mother)?" I questioned. Neither one of us should've had thoughts of fucking because both of us was living with our parents, I was 28 and she was a few years younger than I was but hormones will have you thinking otherwise.

"If my mother's sleep, you can come in," she replied. She stepped out of the vehicle then glided up the steep concrete stairs, within 4-5 minutes I remembered the porch light flicking on and Peanut signaling for me to come from the top of the stairs. I snatched the keys out of the ignition, stepped out of the driver's side then gradually made my way up. Peanut shut and locked the door behind us, then guided me to the couch, which was directly to the right of the door. In front of the sofa was a coffee table with an ashtray full of burnt blunt roaches, cup holders, and two remotes.

"What you want to watch?" Peanut said nearly whispering as she reached for one of the two remotes then turned the television on.

"I don't know, just put something on I hardly watch TV," I replied, which was a true statement. As a writer, all my free time went to fingers dancing on the computer's keyboard. She turned on a random movie on Netflix.

"How about this?" she said placing the remote on the table. I honestly did not give a damn what was playing on the screen. It's was one in the morning, I was borderline sleepy and overly horny. Peanut laid her body against mine resting under my left wing. Before the opening credits of the movie could end, we were face to face, lashing our tongues at one other. I grasped her neck, sliding my tongue down her throat. She wailed quietly almost in silence.

"Pull these down." She said, floundering to unbutton my jeans. I assisted, easily unbuttoning and zipping down the zipper then sliding the pants to the ankle of my shoes. Peanut removed her pants, levitated over my erect dick as she faced my direction, without hurrying she cascaded down my black rod until the tip of me hit rock bottom.

For some reason, sneaky, quiet sex or having sex in places it's possible to get caught is mostly the best. The sense of gambling can give a couple an intensely satisfying rush. Some say shower sex is the best. In my honest opinion, that shit is way overrated. Shower sex feels like I'm fucking nothing but skin and water.

Peanut slowly shifted up and down; the pussy was beyond soaked and gripping me up like a bully. As she enduringly bounced, I felt her inside giving me a feeling that wasn't easy to explain. They say once you do crack, you're instantly addicted because you'll be chasing that same high for the rest of your life. Maybe the pussy had crack in it because right there and then I had thoughts of making her, my woman. As she rode she held her breath and moaned with a close mouth each time she took me fully in. I used the floor for leverage, planting my feet to push up into her. I was reclined back on the sofa; she leaned forward, grasping my face to pull me in for a kiss. Firmly palming her soft booty as she gradually came down and came up at a slow electrifying pace. My manhood was throbbing all in her wetness. Soft moans whispered in my ears, I felt her warm breath on my neck and heard the sound of wet pussy swishing with each stroke that we collided. The speed of her slow bounce decreased even slower, she wrapped her arms around my neck, breathing deeply as I continued to push my feet off the wooden floor. She didn't voice a warning saying nothing considering that she was on the verge of climaxing. She thundered down on me even slower, then slower and slower then seconds later her arms tightened around my neck as her body vibrated like she was having a seizure. She was now cumming all over me. I swayed my hip upward, pushing every inch of this dark chocolate in her interior. No matter how bad she was shaking she still managed to come down and up my pole.

"Cum for me. Cum for me." That's all I needed to hear, those words spoke to my soul. The sound of her pussy, the moans, the incredible feeling in unison spoke to my soul. Within a minute after she came and a second after demanding for me to cum. I became weak, brittle as a twig; in an instant, I lifted her from over top of me as hot cum released, she grasped hold of my manhood then stroked it some more for leftovers. At this moment right here I was vaccinated with my first dose of Lust.

Every day since that arousing Wednesday, we'd fucked two to three times a day. I would come over in the mornings while her mother was at work then leave at 3pm before her mother was en route to come home. In March, I eventually met Peanut's mother. This beautiful cocoa brown elderly lady with locs was the sweetest; the welcome was warmer than baked cookies fresh out the oven. She offered almost the entire kitchen. As March passed, I was over Peanut's house the majority of the day and was rarely at my parents' house. I showed up there just to shower, change clothes, and sleep. My mother gave me a deadline to find my own place by April 20th.

I had the job at the glass factory; the checks were adding up. $350 a week and at this time in my life I had no hustle, I was living check to check. The money I was cashing out wasn't enough for a $650 deposit $650 first and $650 last month's rent. A week before the 20th Peanut suggested that I asked her mother to stay with them until I found a place. This exact day later in the evening, her mother was relaxing on the sofa dress in PJs, and Peanut and I was on the loveseat. We all were watching some show on the television. In my conciseness, I was trying to gather the confidence and the right words to ask Peanut's mother to stay. I never was the person who asked for assistance even back in 2008 when I got terminated from a security job a few days after I signed the lease to an apartment and on top of that a woman I stayed with for a few months burnt all my clothes.

So, I had a handful of some clothes moving in the new place. I could've easily asked my parents for money and rides to interviews but instead, I walked through wet snow with holes in my only pair of shoes and wore three or more hoodies to stay warm. After filling out applications, walking, and catching the bus across Pittsburgh; my socks would be beyond soggy. The outcome of it all, I landed two jobs, bought a car, a nice warm cozy jacket, and a ton of clothes and shoes. Now when hard times hit, I just know there would be better days. I also took more pride in the things I accomplished when I did the shit on my own. I wouldn't ask my own mother for help, what made you think asking someone else mother to live with them felt like? I felt like shit deep inside. Peanut elbowed me in the arm gesturing for me to say something. The pressure was on; if a person can sweat internally, that was me.

"So Mrs. Vicky, I have to ask you something." She turned her attention to me; Peanut also turns her face towards me. Whatever was on the television, the sound seemed to slow down like screwed Houston Hip Hop music.

"Yes, what you have to ask me?" she said with all sweetness but the expression on her face displayed sourness at the same time, maybe because I randomly had a question for her.

"I been searching for an apartment and saving; I have to move out of my parents' house next week. I want to know if it's okay for me to stay for a month until then?" I said speaking rapidly. My question perceived to corner Mrs. Vicky because her only daughter was sitting there, she didn't have to say a word to show she was indecisive.

"If I do let you stay here, you have to sleep alone in the guestroom and pitch in on the groceries." She said still looking unsettled. I stayed in the guest room and was so appreciative that she allowed me to stay. Late nights Peanut sometimes texted me come in here." Or I would tell her, "I'm coming to get some."

I would creep across the wooden squeaking hallway floor to sneak into her room. We had to fuck quietly because her mother's bedroom was literally next door between both of our rooms. As I mentioned before the slow stroking and grinding could be intense when the both of us were putting in an effort to hold all of our sexual emotions inside. We stuffed clothes behind the headboard and the side of the walls to prevent the bed from making noise when penetrating. Now that I matured, I would've obeyed Peanut's mother's rules. She was nice enough to allow me to stay I should have held those hormones in and respected her wishes.

When May came around, I found an apartment; I happened to coach another married couple from Boston and came up on a few dollars. The apartment would not be ready until June 1st so I asked Peanut's mother if I could stay another month, but this time I was less nervous to ask. She agreed that I can stay. When I discovered the place on Craigslist, I asked Peanut to move with me, I couldn't see myself having sex with anyone else and I definitely didn't want her fucking another man. Those were the insecure thoughts. She was fine with moving but only under one condition and that was to be on the lease jointly with me. Now, remember this.

June came around and we moved into the two-bedroom apartment smack dead in the middle of the hood of, Pennsylvania. We moved on one of the main streets where vehicles were passing all hours throughout the day and night, loud cars with banging sound systems, gunshots once or twice a week and people shouting outside at the most random times of the night were frequent sounds. Other than the loud noise outside, the apartment was decent inside, fully carpeted, and felt homely. Moving into this apartment we did not have to sneak around to fuck. Now we were having sex in every room; the kitchen, living room, dining room, the stairway, bathroom, and master bedroom. We produced our own porn movies. When she was in front of the camera, she turned into a whole different type of freak. It's as she was performing to be cast in a special role; she showed the fuck off.

After a two-month cycle of intercourse eventually, we had to get to know each other. You don't know a person until you move in with them. Even in the midst of two months of daily doses of sex, I noticed Peanut couldn't cook. I went from home-cooked meals made from scratch that Patrice prepared to eat bland chicken Alfredo, processed box Hamburger Helpers, boxed mac and cheese, overcooked shrimp, and Grandma's Potato Salad. This is my honest opinion about Grandma's Potato Salad. There's no seasoning in the dish whatsoever, at least sprinkle paprika seasoning on top. There is no sort of black soul in this potato salad. There were several times I would rather wait in the longest lines at Wendy's to avoid eating at home or I would order at a restaurant for take-out then inhale the whole entire meal before parking the car in front of the apartment. When she offered dinner, I would scrap a small portion or I would tell her that I was going to take some food to work with me. I would put food in the container take it as lunch to work then trash the food.

Lust is like a black bag over the head, it will have you blind to the details. The thrilling of pleasure will rob your sight from reality and have you neglect the waving red flags. The black bag was lifted over my head when I was hired to do a driving position; pulling 12 hours a day with one day off during the week and one day off during the weekend. Because I wasn't able to supply her with dick, two to three times a day, which decreased to once a day or sometimes skipped a day or two. She became a different person. The sweet soft talking Peanut's true colors were exposed. I remembered this one day I finished writing a chapter for my second book "Secret Life of the Birds and Bees," I closed the laptop then slid the computer under the couch where I usually sat to write. She damn, near stomped a trail of holes in the floor from the kitchen through the dining room to the living room to demand me to put the machine on the shelf under the TV entertainment center. Peanut did not ask nor give me an explanation. She just demanded that I do so. Now of days, I would have spoken to her calmly and checked her thoroughly, showing no signs of malicious emotions. At this time in my life, she plucked a bitch ass string of nerve that I once had pumping in my vein. We got into a shouting match considering where the computer was and where it should be. This argument went on for a good hour and nothing was settled on her end of the stick. At the end of the day, my shit remained under the couch. If she would have come cordially, I would have been more than welcomed to place the laptop on the shelf. She wanted to wear the pants in the relationship. The problem was that I was not going to kneel down to be her puppet. These demands were coming frequently. "Do the dishes before I get home!" "Take me to the store!"

She even put a time on when we were going to have sex. "We're going to have sex at 6:00 pm." "We're going to have sex before you work." She would arrange. Weekly I accepted this specific broadly. After a week of scheduled fornication, the feeling of sexual tension was not there. It felt like I punching in the clock to a job to have sex. I wasn't as aroused as I was when the intercourse naturally happened. On top of the timed sex, we fucked so much it was 20x harder to make her cum. My rule is to never leave a woman without making her cum; so, there were times I would eat her pussy for 30 minutes straight to have her climax.

As time went on her true colors got brighter, one night after driving home I caught a glimpse of Peanut getting out of a truck a couple blocks away from home. Peanut caught the bus to work and back, most days I would pick her up. This exact day she said she would catch the bus home. I hurried into the apartment so she couldn't spot me. I grasped a hold of my laptop, laid on the couch, kicked my shoes off then pretended to write. I heard keys at the door turning. She pushed the door open then walked in.

"Hey, babe." She politely said with butterflies flying out her mouth.

"Hey what's up? How was your day?" I said glaring back at Peanut's exhausted face with her thick hair in a ponytail as she leaned against the loveseat to remove the black work shoes. She stood up to come toward me. I sat my open laptop on the tan carpet floor as she went in for a kiss before sitting beside me. In my consciousness, I was hoping she didn't give a man oral before pressing her lips against mine. This thought circled my mind a million times while she sat beside me.

"How was the bus ride home?" I asked.

"Why are you asking?" she was suspicious/

"Because it's been a while since you caught the bus home."

"Oh yeah, it was the same as before. The bus came a little later than what I expected or I would have had you come get me." She said each and every word with a straight face.

"So the bus dropped you off down the street in a black truck too?" I said swiping her off the couch like a spider on the leg.

"That was my friend Lisa. She picked me up from work." She changed the storyline instantly. Since that day, I made a vow to not pick her up from work again.

The last straw the broke the camel's back was the day she came home at 4am after getting off work at 7pm. While waiting for Peanut to come home she texted me once and it read, "I love you." Flashbacks of walking in on Patrice with another man haunted me after receiving the "I love you" text. I texted multiple times and called to no answer. Four in the morning came along she crept in the door, tip-toed up the stairwell then laid beside me. My eyes were open wide glaring at the silhouette on the wall of the electric wires outside the window from the orange street lights. I was so hurt I couldn't cry, I just knew from here on out I don't give a flying fuck. I slept with the neighbor across the street, the neighbor that I used to date next door. I began to host clubs, now more women were pouring in, and I even had a threesome all while I showed up at home and still loved on Peanut. I was literally abusing myself trying to cover up the pain all at the same time. The biggest mistake was sleeping with Patrice.

My father told me, "Never sleep with your baby mother. She can resurface feelings. She may be cool for a while but when you're not hitting or you're dealing with someone else she'll be even more possessive." I didn't listen to the old man. I had to find out myself. The day I slept with Patrice I accidentally went to sleep butt-ass naked laying in the bed with a wet rag covering my dick. She took a photo and threatened to send the picture to Peanut if I denied sleeping with her. Patrice blackmailed me for a month until I had enough.

"Go ahead and send it," I said, in my mind, I'm thinking she didn't have the heart to send the photo to her.

The next night all my belongings were sitting outside the house in garbage bags, she changed the locks, changed her phone number, and blocked me from all social media. The confusing thing of all this was why did Peanut keep the kid's electric car.

The moral of the story, don't allow amazing sex to keep you stuck in a web of lust. If you feel yourself falling for someone because of the undeniable sex, take a step back, clear your mind and get to know them. Sex is important but without that how is the connection? To be honest, sometimes an intriguing conversation laughs, and smiles can feel better than sex.

009. Dose of Love

On the chilly night of November 3rd, 2017 not in a million years did I think this day would come. Me, Sex Symbol Tink, the ladies' man himself was gearing up to propose. I guess you could say that the pigs were flying this day because I was in awe. How did this happen? My close friends and family couldn't believe this either. When a man is truly in love, all the other women become irrelevant. A man will only be faithful to someone he can't see himself without. At this time, I couldn't. Days before the proposal I asked Brittany's father for permission to marry his daughter while Brittany's beautiful mother sat beside him and listened, sitting on the sofa across me. The single lamp nearly glowed in the corner of the living room gave the scenery a calming mood.

"Why you want to marry Brittany?" Her father asked with squinted eyes. I simply responded without a nervous bone.

"Because I can't see myself without her." In the past, I was guilty of telling women that I couldn't see them with someone else but there was a big difference in not seeing yourself without someone. Mothers, fathers, uncles, aunties, brothers, sisters, cousins, and friends about 30 people gathered on the opened second-floor garage, gazing down with shiny confetti in hands; ready to throw it if Brittany said "yes" to the proposal. The garage was directly across the street from Brittany's hair salon downtown. I was on the ground floor standing outside of the garage, across the street with my friend Carlos holding my phone recording live on social media. The parking attendant allowed me to use the garage, I had a photographer ready to catch the moment, and I couldn't forget about the breathtaking vocalist Cam Chamber who sang when she came out. Random individuals were standing around; observing the elaborate scene.

Standing there holding my breath. My legs felt like noodles, my body was numb and my heart was beating a million miles per second. Nervous was an understatement. I kept dipping into my pocket to feel the ring. This was my way of knowing this was real. It was my version of pinching myself to detect that this was not a dream. At the time, I was literally taking the first step of marrying my dream woman. I was dressed in black slim jeans, a black sweater, a blue jean jacket with some dark wooden brown boots from ALDO.

"Are you ready? My boy." Carlos said holding the phone recording.
"Yes," I replied smiling, still feeling jittery.
"My boy Tink about to get married."

"I know bra. Who would've thought it would come to this."

No longer than a split second after I spoke the heavy glass door swung open. A stylist that worked in the salon exited the building first. Next, was Brittany.

"Oh I will (stay with you) through the ups and the downs
Yes I will (stay with you) gotta stay when no one else is around
And when the dark clouds arrive
I will stay by your side
And I know we'll be alright..." Cam Chambers covered the song "Stay with me." One of John Legend's classic love songs.

Brittany walked across the street coming towards me with astonishment written all over her face. Abruptly reality seemed to slow down, the outside noise became silent and the thumping of my heart was beating so hard that I could hear it internally. She stepped onto the curb, promptly I grasped her left hand. Every word that I rehearsed day and night for this special moment was completely erased. The delightful words that I'd written wouldn't spill out. This was when everything came to normal. The background noise, Cam singing, the camera flashing, and Brittany standing in front of me. I took a deep breath and swallowed whatever nervous saliva I had in my throat. Then I spoke. Accumulating words that I felt.

"Since the day that I met you I knew deep inside you were the one. I never thought I would ever experience the true feeling of love. I want to live this feeling for the rest of my life and build a strong foundation between the two of us." I pulled the box out of my pocket, kneeled to the concrete on one knee. Brittany covered her face in disbelief probably feeling a wave of thrilling emotions.

"Brittany, can you marry me?" I said, glaring up, holding her hand as I slid the right on the finger.

"Oh my goodness, yes," she wept. "Oh, my goodness." She repeated repeatedly. The crowd on the second-floor hovered and applauded, screaming and praising us. The shiny gold and silver flacks of confetti glittered in the night light as it rained on our heads. Glaring up at the confetti, twinkle and glitter made me think of how we got to this moment.

October 14th, 2014: **The Meet and Greet.**

Patricia and I had split apart for almost a week. After the club, I went to an after-hour function in Oakland near Pitt University. The place was exceedingly packed shoulder to shoulder. Near the end of closing the DJ slowed the environment down with modern-day R&B Records.

Trey Songz "Touching" seeped through the speakers. I remembered couples and non-couples grabbing partners like a high school dance. All the women were cuffed. It was like musical chairs but the women were the chairs. Soon as the slow jams played all the men grabbed the hands of a woman. I was the one without, the loner, the guy on his way to the wall. Before I could become beached at the wall. The people on the dance floor seemed to split like the Red Sea creating a clear lane. There she was in all black, standing alone at 5'5 with silky bouncing reddish hair; her ends were three inches past her shoulders. She wore burgundy lipstick painted across her lips camouflaging the wine-colored hair. She must've felt my eyes beaming into her soul. The split second she caught my attention she gazed in my direction then gazed into my pupils. My consciousness spoke to me loud and clear telling me to approach her. Maybe it was God, maybe the inner me. Nevertheless, my heart pointed in the direction she was standing. Without thought, I stepped through the open lane to come near this dream woman. She was standing there swaying gently to the music. I'm one hundred percent sure, she was prepared for me to say something. Women can feel a man's desires, even if he chickens out and doesn't speak. I believe most women know if they're going to give the man a chance or not before he even speaks a word.

"Hey. I couldn't help but to say something," I said with butterflies' ricocheting throughout my body all while I kept a straight composure and spoke with all the confidence.

"My name is Darren. It's nice to meet you." I continued as I stretched my arm to reach for her hand to shake.

"I'm Brittany."

"I'm not the best dancer, but I would mind trying to just to dance with you."

"I can't either so that makes two of us." She admitted with a slight smile.

"We can at least two-step." I crept behind and continued speaking near her ear while we stepped on each other toes. I asked about her age, birthday, and profession. She answered 29, she was a year older than me, a Gemini, and she stated that she was a hairstylist. That verified why Brittany's hair was perfectly styled. I mentioned that I wrote erotic novels, my age and assured her that Leo's were the best sign out of all of the zodiacs. We talked on other topics briefly as the songs changed twice. Eventually, we exchanged numbers before departing the dancefloor.

Me and her met up a week later at a bar in Mount Washington. In the bar, Brittany and I was surrounded by drunk white people. Despite the old rock and country music, we laughed throughout the whole entire night, took back several shots of Fireball Whiskey with the bartenders and the surrounding cool white people. This first night confirmed that she was my soulmate, the homie. The energy, the connection between the both of us was undeniable so impossible to deny that some drunken white lady complimented us and said we were the cutest couple. Then the boyfriend of the woman blessed us with another round of Fireball.

"This is to the beautiful couple." We all drank in unison.

This one date sticks out to me the most. At this nasty chicken restaurant on the west side, we sat for hours sharing our goals and ideas. I asked her when she first began to do hair, how did she build her clientele? She mentioned that she stood outside downtown in front of hair salons she was working at and passed cards to women walking past for hours. She had a blowout, cut and style special on Tuesdays called Britt Tuesdays for $25. After the first experience, everyone became a client. Within months her book began to overflow with clients craving to get their hair did. She said owners and contracted stylists turned on her when consumers of all professions stampeded through the doors. Brittany mentioned she moved from one hair salon to another. One salon fired her because she was using too much water with the number of people she was bringing in. She ended by saying her desire was to build a fancy upscale salon. It was going to be a steady peaceful sanctuary for not just the clients but for herself as well. I believed every word she uttered. I had big faith.

Me, I voiced that I had goals of writing an Amazon and New York bestseller, I brought up that I wanted to own a carpet cleaning franchise. I told her someday I wouldn't have to lift a finger. She praised me giving me nothing but positive vibes. She had me knowing that this dream of mine would come true.

We mainly met at bars and low-key restaurants over two weeks. We never spent time on the weekends except for this one weekend. Shortly I had a visit from a woman I had slept with in the past after leaving a club. She was the last resort. Fuckable and not too bad looking. I called Brittany earlier in the day several times before deciding to make an appearance in a club. We were supposed to meet in the evening since she was kid-free. The whole entire day I didn't receive a text or call; nothing stating that the plans were canceled. The result was me being stripped to my boxer briefs with this woman with sexual thirstiness to fuck me because the last time we had sex was magical. She rapidly kissed all over my neck, chest, and down to my pelvis and nearly was about to pull my hard blackness out the cage.

"Let me get comfortable before I do this." She said rolling off the bed. I was hot and ready. If arousal was air and I was a balloon I would've been fully blown.

"I been wanting you for a while now. Are you still with your girlfriend?" She was referring to Patrice as she lifted her shirt from over her head.

"Nah we're not together," I said nonchalantly, I honestly was not trying to talk about anything. I was yearning for her to place her mouth over top of me.

"Aww, I'm sorry to hear. Ya'll seemed so happy." She said with artificial sympathy, as she slid her pants along with her panties down to the floor. Without delay, the air in my aroused balloon deflated. A waft of a bad batch of sour mildew pussy was the needle to pop whatever erotic thought I had. The smell was so loud, it was yelling, it was crying. It stank so badly that I was desperate to find a way out. Saved by the bell. My phone rang. I reached over to the floor, snagged my pants to get a hold of the phone in my pocket. The ringing stopped. It was a missed call from Brittany.
"Hold on a second." I scooted off the bed as she climbed on the bed naked.
"I have to make this call it's important." I swiftly went into the bathroom then called back.
"Hey what's up I got your call."

"Sorry about earlier what you doing now. You can come over if you want?" The "You can come over if you want" were the words that canceled all the bad thoughts I had after being stood up. It was past 2am. Never in my life had I visited a woman's house after 12 am and not had sex. Trailing the short breather of fresh air in the bathroom, I returned to the funky bedroom. I grasped my pants and hurriedly slid them on.

"Hey, I have to handle something. I can come back in the morning. We can get breakfast." The lies were spilling out my lips like drinking water from a water fountain. In a heartbeat, I was out the door, in my car following the GPS to Brittany's house.

It was late when she texted me minutes before pulling up that the door was open. When I came into the house, the corner lamp in between the sofa and the living room window was barely beaming.

"I'm back here." She announced, I strolled through the short hall passing a bathroom to the right and the kitchen to the left to stepping into a fully furnished medium-sized bedroom. Brittany was tucked under the covers, her face buried in the pillow.

"You're all sleep," I said standing there glaring down at her a bit dumbfounded on what I should do. She lifted her head, gazed at me for a split second with squinted eyes. Then her face fell back into the dent of the pillow.

"What are you doing? Are you going get in the bed?" She asked.

"Oh, yeah." I slid down my pants and removed the hoodie I wore over the t-shirt. I was a bit unsettled. This woman had me acting strange. If she was any other woman I would've been hopping dead in the bed without second thoughts. With just boxer briefs and a t-shirt on I crawled in the bed then laid beside the slumped body.

My conciseness was getting the best of me. I came to be puzzled about what I should do considering that she was half-sleep. All in the same time, she sporadically pushed her ass against my manhood. Yet I was still overly thinking about how I should utilize my hands to get her stimulated. I also had thought of just letting her sleep peacefully. Unsure I placed my hand on her naked thigh and caressed it to catch her reaction. She scooted back against me some more. The drawback gave me a limited extent of confidence. I dragged my hands near her inner thighs, touching them firmly. She scooted some more. I reached in between her thighs and traced the outside of the thin boy shorts. I was surprised she was drenched. I located her love button then rub in a circular motion with my index and middle as the wetness seeped out of the thin material. She applied her hand against mines so I could rub deeper against the gummy. Brittany released mild wails as my fingers stirred her juices. Her reaction gave me enough confidence to duck under the sheets to free her shorts from her legs. She was at her sexual peak; there was no need to foreplay. This time I didn't bless the entrée I just devoured.

During the moment of intercourse, it was different from the feeling I felt for any woman in the past. For the last couple of weeks before thoughts of sex our spirit, the ambiance, the quality of our vibe aligned so well it seemed like we knew each other for years. So, when we slept together that was just the icing on the cake with the sprinkles and ice cream on the side. It was not just sex or a piece of pussy with a pretty face I accomplished fucking. It was more profound than lust, the rush of new pussy, or relief of sexual frustration. The combination of being on a deeper soul level blended with mind-blowing intimacy created a special bliss.

This one afternoon I brought Brittany's lunch to the salon she worked. The salon was packed with women. There were clients in each station, some standing and some sitting in the waiting room. If their eyes were darts with metal tips, I would be filled with more holes than a dartboard. Soon as I left the salon doors after delivering the food I received a text from Patrice. It had been almost four weeks since Patrice and I had spoken. We would text considering what our child needed or pick-up times. Other than that, there were no conversations.

"Oh, you're dropping off food to bitches." Whoever was in the salon sent a message to Patrice in a double. I was not able to feel the cool breeze of the beginning of November before receiving this disturbing message.

Women seem to care when a man is serious about someone or when there is competition. If I posted an intimate or just a regular photo with a woman on social media right now. I guarantee women I haven't spoken to in the past will resurface, the women who have been playing games will submit themselves and the women with crushes will finally confess their feelings.

Years later when I proposed to Brittany the floodgates full of thirsty women broke through the cracks. I admit I was one of the men along with a million others who drowned in the women currents.

The same day that I delivered the food, Patrice began sending threatening messages to Brittany. She threatened to come to the salon and fight her on sight. She sent delusional statements like "You took him away from his family." There were so many more threats, over thirty messages to be exact. Brittany screenshot all messages then sent them all to me. Trailing this particular day Brittany began to distance herself, we hung out but not as much, we talked but not as often. Our friendship, our bond was shedding like a snake.

Weeks later, past midnight I was lying in bed as the streetlights peeked through the blinds. The phone screen brightened the room with Brittany's face on display as it vibrated on the nightstand. I barely spoke to Brittany within the past couple of days so when she called I was surprised.

"Hey what's up? Stranger." I said, not trying to sound sleepy.

"Hey, Darren." Her voice was low and dry as sandpaper.

"Everything okay," I said with concern.

"We can't do this anymore." The words cracked out her vocal box, she seemed like she didn't want to utter these words. Like when a parent whoops their child and hurts the parent more than the child is taking in the pain.

"What you mean?" I asked. At this time, my heart felt like it was getting chopped in a blender.

"You have too much going on. You have three kids. How would you be able to take care of someone else? Then the drama with your baby mother. It's too much for me."

"So you're telling me. It's over?" I had to confirm. She paused for a slight second. I'm not sure if she was crying or putting more thought into the answer.

"Yes. I was talking to someone. They said it would be best for me."

.

"This is what you want? "My heart was a smoothie by now. An outside source of our bond had got between and planted a seed, which was true. At this time, I didn't have the financial resources to take care of myself, Brittany, her child, and my children. She was completely right.

"Yes, Darren. We can still be friends."
"Okay. I'm fine with that."

Right after that conversation, I went backward then got back with Patrice. This was the biggest mistake. Never go back unless both of your hearts are in it.

I caught Patrice in bed two months later. Got into a new lustful relationship with Peanut. I was blackmailed by Patrice; she sent the photos to Peanut. Then May of 2016 Brittany and me reunited.

010. The Storm Before Settling

The month of April 2016

House Keys

My right handcuffed firmly around Faith's throat while she was bent over sending her natural jiggly round booty at me in front of the sink in the powder room. The vanity strip lights shined bright above our reflection in the mirror. Thrusting all of me, without a fuck giving into this thick juicy redbone I watched her facial expression transform and her blond wig shift wildly in the mirror as she took every inch of penetration from my long black hardness. I literally met Faith in a club I hosted every Wednesday while I was dating Peanut. When Peanut changed the locks to the place where my name was on the lease and when my mother said "figure it out, you can't live here" to avoid living on the streets or sleeping in my car I went into survival mode and exchanged dick for house keys and a comfortable bed to sleep in. I had the money to move into a new place. I was in the process of searching and getting approved for an apartment and the process dragged.

My pants down at my ankles, I was biting my bottom lip, brutally drilling this dick in her rear to dig a tunnel to her heart. Her long fingernails swiped across the sink; knocking over the toothbrush holder, the hand soap, and a scattering of bathroom possession as her moans escaped from each stroke I launched inside her.

"Yes, yes, yes daddy." I pulled Faith by the throat into a standing position her spine moved closer to my chest.

"Cum on this dick. Nasty bitch" I demanded, whispering in her ear while her saturated pussy absorbed the lengths of me pounding her back in. At the time, she attempted to respond I let loose of her throat then slid every finger but the thumb deep in her mouth. Straight away tears cascaded down her yellow face, her moans became muffled. I continued to apply in and out in repeat at a thunderous rhythm all as I swayed my hips for the perfect stroke. My fingers soaked, saliva rolling down my forearm as she slobbed on my hand like a nibbling toy. The muffled moans increased as she slightly bit down on my fingers. Soon as I felt her teeth clamping tighter I immediately let loose. All the words she wanted to speak fumbled out clearly.

"I'm cumming, I'm cumming, fuck, I'm cumming." She voiced as her legs became uncontrollably shaky. Unexpectedly a spray of water shot down Faith's thighs like a power washer. The poor rug on the floor got all the mist. Her rain didn't stop my thunder. I kept striking, striking, and striking. An electrifying shock traveled through the body. I ripped the condom off

"Get on your knees" I demanded. She turned around, falling to the watered rug. She stretched her tongue out. Her eyes desperately begged me to ejaculate in her mouth. "Ummm Ummm" I groaned as I unmanageably drizzled myself over her face. Faith invited me over daily, she knew my situation I didn't beg, ask or plant a seed to stay. She wanted some reliable penis and a relationship. I told her I was not fit for a relationship. She ignored the fact that I wasn't for commitment and still gave me the keys to her place.

Then there was Maria, an Indian woman I met at Whole Foods while waiting in line at the food bar. Maria stood in front of me with a white V-neck elbow shirt, brown loosen boho pants, and some brown Birkenstock sandals. Maria's skin was the tone of creamy cocoa butter, her straight hair ended in the middle of her spine. She was 5'6 and more or less than 110 pounds. In her exotic graceful face, she could pass for a woman in the late 20's but judging by the way she dressed I knew she was older. There were at least 6 to 7 people in front of us. I asked Maria if she tried the honey-glazed salmon, just to spark a conversation to kill time. The shiny glazed salmon behind the glass was looking intriguing so I asked.

I had no intentions on making a move to show any interest. She replied

"No, I haven't, I'm allergic to seafood." I kind of felt bad.
"So no seafood," I asked, shaking my head in disbelief. She went on a told me a youth story on the time she consumed a piece of shrimp. She described the throat closing, short breathing the facial outbreak, and the rushed trip to the hospital. She informed me that she was a vegetarian.

"How can you do it, I can't eat salad and grass all day." I joked. She let out a soft laugh. I didn't think she thought my fooling around was amusing.

"That's not all we eat. There's Tofu, chickpeas, and a whole bunch of substitutes for meat."

"Let's do a lunch date at a vegetarian restaurant someday. You find the place and I'll pay." I pitched. Maria's eyes widened. She seemed quite dazed that I inquired to take her out.

"Excuse me? What's your name and how old are you?" she said as the line moved a bit.
"I'm 29 and my name is Darren."
"I'm 41 that would not be a good idea. I have 12 years on you."

"It's a friendly foodie date. Nothing farther than that. Maybe you can convert me into a vegetarian." These words were the power punch. *Convert me into a vegetarian*. She changed her mind in a hurry. One thing about vegetarians they will move the world to stop someone from eating animals.

"I know this one place."

In that same week, we met for lunch. The menu was puzzling. I had no idea what the dishes were with the lentils, seitan, spelt, and a ton of bean foods. I picked the Tofu. That was the only thing on the list I had heard of even though I never tried it.

When I chewed into the rubbery tofu I almost coughed up a lung by gagging on the silky chewy texture. January of 2020 I became a Pescatarian. I still have no desire on eating Tofu. I had rice, sweet potatoes, and green beans for the side, which I ate.

During the lunch, Maria mentioned that she was a travel DNP, she was divorced, no kids, she labeled her dog as a child. She hadn't dated anyone in three years since her ex-husband. The conversation we held was inspiring. Maria owned multiple properties, traveled the world, and finished school after her parents died in a car accident. She offered to front the bill. I denied and paid, even though the veggie lunch was beyond expensive.

At the end of lunch, Maria invited me over for Sunday dinner. The night of dinner Maria's mood was entirely different; she was furthermore talkative and exceedingly friendly. On top of everything, Maria's appearance did not match the innocent nurse I had met the past two times. Maria was on fire with her red silky dress, red lipstick, and hair tied in a bun.

Maria gave me a tour around the townhouse she owned. It was three levels tall with high ceilings and new appliances in the kitchen. I followed up the fully carpeted steps through the hallways to each room and bathroom floor by floor. In the middle of touring, I caught a glimpse of Maria giving me a seductive glare and scanning me from head to toe. Last but not least was the master bedroom. This room was equipped with a king-size bed, humongous television hanging on the wall along paintings with a ton of colors. There was a huge walk-in closet with clothes scattered on the floor and several outfits on the hangers. What caught my attention the most was the enormous master bathroom. The oversized Scarface Jacuzzi, the walk-in glass shower, and the marble sink were incredible. After admiring the bathroom, we made our way back to her bedroom.

"Hey, I have a question," I said before she could take a step down the stairs.

"Yes, I have answers."

"Why you keep giving me this look."

"What look?" She said playing dumb.

"The look you been giving me since time I been here."

"You caught me? Oh gosh." she paused for a split second then continued.

"You are a sexy chocolate man. This is the first time in my life that I have actually been alone with one. I wish you were a few years older."

"What age have to do with it? I'm grown. Age is just a date with numbers on the day we were born" Then I continued "Matter fact Come here." I relished. She came forward with doubt in each step towards me on the carpet floor. I grasped her wrist then planted multiple gentle kisses on her hand; trailing my juicy lips to her wrist to the forearms. Her arm became light as a feather as I pecked.

Hand kisses will send goosebumps through a woman's body. It may send a throbbing signal to the vagina as well.

Maria was sucked into my caressing touch. Her glossy eyes were bagging for more affection as she breathed calmly. When I released her hand from my grasp, we peered into one another's eyes for no longer than thirty seconds. We both went in for a kiss standing at the foot end of the bed. We began with a few pecks then our tongues awkwardly tangled or should I say slapped. Maria was not the greatest kisser. There was much passion in our kissing. I was slightly thrown off because her tongue slid quickly from side to side with no rhythm. Her kissing technique did not align with the stroke of my love language. I matched her speedy tongue swinging then leaned forward to drive her back to the mattress.

I detached my mouth from hers then landed kisses on her neck. Whatever perfume she wore had a warm flowery spice. Each individual kiss that butterflied against her neck she swiveled as she took deep breaths with shut eyes and an open mouth. My lips trailed to the collar down to the shoulders, all while I slipped the shoulder strap down on the gown to exposing her perfectly plump C cup breast. The areola around her hardened nipple reminded me of a Reese's Cup. I clamped my lips around then sucked tenderly while my tongue danced upon the nipple. I reached between her thighs, slid whatever color panties to the side, and placed my index and middle fingers over her clit. As I persisted to suck, I massaged her love button in a ponderous circular motion. I could've sworn she climaxed within 30 seconds. Her body stiffened as I watched her back arch from the mattress. Her moans remained soft although the breathing increased. My fingers were drizzling with her juices all over.

I ducked low then buried my face in her pussy Coated my kissers around her clitoris and like I've done in previous stories I painted the button with my tongue. Sliding the tongue side to side caused her chest to rise and fall alternately as she breathed deeply in and out. Tongue dancing sliding and sliding, stimulating the clit. The juices of her pussy poured down my lips, drizzling down my beard; giving my chin hairs a glorious shine. Abruptly she stopped breathing, her soft moans paused for about five seconds. Silence took over the room. All that was heard was the clamping sounds of me devouring the pussy as if it was my last meal. Within that five seconds, I swung my tongue side to side with a saliva-filled mouth. Her body stiffened again. Once the five seconds ended she released moans, exhaled the oxygen she held in, and climaxed all over my lips. She grasped hold of the back of my head pushing my face deeper between her thighs. Her legs were trembling out of control as I continued to lick. I literally had thoughts of eating her box until she passed out.

"Oh my gosh, oh my gosh here I, here I, cum again." She wailed this time screaming. "Oh gosh, oh gosh. I'm cummin" Her body severely tensed then flopped as she let loose of everything and blessed me with more of her essences.

As she laid there in shock, attempting to regain possession of her twitching soul. I hurried, removing all my clothes including my socks. I assisted and stripped the red dress to expose her naked body. In the time, I positioned myself on the bed with a hard-stiff hook dick. Maria's eyes widen, swiftly she reached down to stroke my thickness.

"It's so big and black." She repeated three or four times as she stroked my ego. Soon as she unshackled my hard blackness, I separated her legs apart, leaned forward then buried my tongue in her mouth. I grabbed hold of my manhood then slowly plugged myself inside.

Most of the time when a woman says she hasn't had sex or dated more than a year, normally I don't believe them. I was completely convinced. Maria's love box was tighter than a balled first but juicy and slippery as a fresh peach.

I inched my way in moderately. Each inch deeper, I felt her arms tighten around my back and her breath tickle my neck as she moaned. Once all inches' touched the bottom, I repeated and inched my way down. The third time I gradually pushed this black dick down. I felt her body intensify once again. I knew she was on the verge of climaxing. It was all a repeat of when she stopped breathing and moaning during oral. The fourth stroke I swayed in at a mild pace and dived in deeply. The fifth stroke deep down inside she clenched her arms around tighter, slicing the flesh on my back as her thighs shook like a steering wheel in a vehicle with a bad wheel bearing. Her moans scattered and echoed through the high ceilings. The sixth stroke I held my dick in the depth of her to make her cum even harder.

I moved my chest from Maria's to reposition myself. Knees on the mattress, upper body in a vertical extent with her legs relaxing on my shoulder and her feet dangling. All over again I began to operate this time a bit faster. In and out I stroked. In and out my black long blackness is sailing through her wetness. No longer than five minutes, she was climaxing again. We went someone more; she came within another five minutes. Stacking orgasms again and again. This woman couldn't stop cummin.

"Ride this dick," I said as I pulled my manhood out of her cummentator. My pole had a shiny glare, glimmering from the gloss of her fluids. I flopped back on the bed, resting my head on the nearest pillow. Maria hovered over top of me then gasped for air as she glided down slowly.

"It's so big and black" she uttered between short breaths. Getting rode was the only way I could cum at this point. The chances of myself cumin were slim, each time she climaxed she crawled back which reset the excitement of having an orgasm. She rooted her hand on my chest then began to bounce her whole entire body on me. I had to acknowledge Maria's riding performance was not supreme. Just as a man should sway his waist when penetrating a woman, a woman has to sway her hips as well when she's bouncing the box on the dick. Her shoulders were awkwardly shrugging; her back was shifting in and out and her titties had a slight bounce. Again, no longer than 60 seconds she dug her claws into my chest.

"It's so big, it's so big," she said as I planted my feet in the mattress. I shifted my waist upward, held both hands on her little booty full of stretch marks then hammered up like putting a nail in the ceiling. As I lifted my waist inside I pushed her ass down on me for firm thrusts.

As I constantly drove up, she leaned toward me then began to slithering her tongue in my open mouth. Every stroke that I conducted I felt that I was near eruption. Even though I couldn't see the dick sliding within her wet walls. I could visualize it sliding up and down, I could feel her tight pussy gripping the bulk of this black stick, I could feel her breathing, her butter-soft skin flourishing against my body, I could hear her light moans and feel her long hair sweeping on my neck. As she fell down on me I felt my penis getting extremely harder. She became tense then I followed. We both were stiffer than cardboard.

"Keep going I'm about to cum." I declared. I grasped her ass securely then pushed her deep. So, deep, if she was sitting up you would be able to witness a dick print in her stomach. All in the same time, she melted all over me as I hurried to lift her off the top of me to shoot a mega load all over her ass. We ate, watched a movie then fucked again.

After this day, Maria became beyond clingy. She was obsessed with being with a dark man. She called me her chocolate man out of heaven. She called me more than ten times a day. She accommodated me with gifts almost every time I visited. She offered money, always ordered food and she gave me a key to her townhouse. Maria would've been the perfect woman for someone who loved the extra attention. No matter how much she spoiled me, the clinginess had me on edge. No amount of money could have me fall for anyone.

Through April, I was between Faith's place, Maria's house, and a couple others all while I was searching for an apartment. At the end of the month, I was approved for an apartment in Turtle Creek Pa. A couple days before getting approved Britany surprisingly texted me.
"Hey."

This one text changed me in so many ways. We planned a date. Britany's boyfriend had broken up with her and a month before Peanut locked me out of my apartment. We both were single. We messaged on special occasions on social media in the middle of our relationship but nothing further than Happy Birthdays and congratulations to her on owning a salon. Although she abruptly cut me off the face of the Earth two years earlier, she still had a tiny spot in my heart. For the fact that I knew someone persuaded her to let go, I was willing to accept whatever apology and give us a second chance.

The first day we spent the whole entire day together. We ate at a burger spot, went to play dodgeball at the trampoline park then caught a movie after. Days later, I signed the lease to the new apartment. I fucked Maria one more time and Faith once again. Once I had the keys to my place, I knew for sure Britany was my soulmate. I simply told every woman I was dealing with that I needed some space for myself. They all respected my wishes but Maria. She cried over the phone, poured her heart out to me. She tried to offer pussy, money, gifts, and more. I didn't want anything. Following the date with Britany, we were together every day until our breakup.

011. Commitment

Some people are put in your life to make you a better person and to expand your mind and look beyond the horizon. No matter how long or short the relationship lasted. Every relationship will leave a mark.

May of 2016: **The commitment.**

In the beginning, all relationships seem too good to be true. The first six months are amazing, depending on who you're with. Some people will show their true cards within a week. Britany and I reconnected like we never fell off. The chemistry between us was genuine, fun, and respectable. Just like that, we jumped right into a relationship trailing our second date.

The salon was our personal bar at night. There were many nights we sat in the spinning chairs under the bright salon lights and drank wine, fooled around, and vibing to old school R&B music until 2 to 3am. If not at the salon we were somewhere eating.

On this drunk night coming from a restaurant, we battled song for song; competing to play the best 90's and 2000's tracks. Master P's "Make Em Say", DMX's "Lose My Mind" Project Pat's "Chicken Head." were a few of the songs I played. Shine's "Bad Boyz" Young Jeezy's "Air Forces" were her choices of songs. When she put on Lil Wayne's "Cash Money Millionaire" we sang word for word in unison *"I got a bitch in the back, got a hoe in the front, one cookin the crack, one rollin the blunt. You get pussy and ass from a beautiful broad. If you looking for that, holla at ya boy, I'm a m- m-mack mack A p-p-pimp."* We were in the vehicle getting hype to every song we picked. The energy was on a hundred. Head bobbing, dancing, glaring at one another while we sang lyrics to all songs. The affection level was on an all-time high in public engagement. Grocery store runs we danced. In the middle of chips and snacks aisles, I've got twerked on as the store's music played on the loudspeaker. We were living free and living a love story.

June came upon us, within the entire month of May I slept at my apartment practically for two weeks. The remainder of the days I dwelled at Britany's place. On her birthday, a couple days into June I organized a surprise bowling birthday party. All her loved ones came through and rented bowling shoes to celebrate a Gemini's born date. When Britany walked into the alley, she was more than ecstatic. As I got a load of how much she relished and cherished the moments with lots of smiles, laughs, cheers, and drinks during the party I felt a tremendous sensation of great pleasure. When a man, woman, a loved one, or someone that's into you gets a genuine thrill of making you feel special. This is the person that you want in your corner. This is the person that never wants to witness you fail. Unfortunately, when I think of it. That's not always true though. Some people will also manipulate you by showing you differently, give you all the butterflies that you never felt, give you the electrifying experience or buy you a gift that will touch your heart then be fraudulent and misleading for their own gain.

Brief example before I continue the story while this is on my mind.

Summer of 2020 I had a long-distance situation with a woman in New York. We met at a Herbalife convention in New Orleans a year earlier. Before she came to visit me, she observed my social media to pinpoint the attaching possessions I posted. She noticed a ton of elephant canvas and elephant ornaments scattered in the background of my photos. She bought acceptable elephants gifts that fit perfectly in my place. She went as far as asking me for my children's ages and randomly sending kids' clothes to my apartment. We flew back and forward From NY to Pa. The sex we had was amazing and the affiliation was at a good standard. As our situation began to grow, she admitted that she had a sponsor in another state. Her sponsor was a white man she pretended to date for years. He literally paid for everything from car notes, insurance, the high ass New York City rent, and money in her pockets. Whatever she desired. The downside was she had answered his Facetime calls day and at night, she had to deal with him when he was emotional the arguments. All the stressful shit that comes with being in a relationship. To make a long story short she dared to ask me to Cashapp her $200 every Friday when I got paid. Even if I were a millionaire, I wouldn't do that dumb shit. No telling how many others she was juicing for money. If I didn't know about her situation with the sponsor, of course, I would assist with a bill if needed. After that conversation, she was cut that day.

Back to the story.

Following the party, we stumbled into her dark house drunk. So intoxicated we didn't bother to flip the lights on or lock the front door. The cheap alcohol that was given at the open bar in the bowling alley did not bring a halt to us feeling all over one another. Falling and kissing up the stairs to the master room where we swiftly removed our clothes. When we first reunited, she told me she was practicing celibacy. She did not want to have sex until she was with someone for a year or married. I respected her wishes and had not had sex the whole month of May after I fucked Maria and Faith at the very beginning. 30 days may not seem like a lot of days to a woman but to most men, they'll lose their fucking mind.

Our connection was so dope, the sex didn't matter. She was the homie but just more intimate. If the person you're loving is the homie first before anything. I could put money that the relationship was going to last long.

In anticipation of sliding her panties off, I glared up after dropping kisses over her entire body.
"Are you sure you want to do this?" I simply asked.

"Yes, I am sure." She clarified. That was all I need to hear. I separated the underwear away from her body pronto, went down a pleased her orally. The rest of the night, we rolled naked in between the covers, shuffling passion that intertwined with our spirits. Sunday morning, we were back at it, making love as the sunshine peeked through the window and the birds chirped their beaks. She desired to fornicate from sun up to sun down and we were both under the influence. She yearned to feel the real emotions, the real rush of our powers colliding; she craved for me to refresh her memory now that she was sober. It was my honor to grant what she wished for.

A month later, Britany sent me on a scavenger hunt a couple days before my birthday in July. On a Wednesday, my day off she sent me a text while she was at the gym.

"I left something on the kitchen table."
I checked the kitchen table and peeped a card with a letter inside. It read. Something in this matter. "How much she loved me, how she appreciated me. She mentioned that she knows how busy of a man I am with the kids and the stressful job. At the end of the letter, there was an address, it instructed to be at the place at 1PM. I followed the GPS to Centre Avenue in Shady Side. I scrolled through the glass door of a massage parlor.

"You must be Darren." I was surprised by a masseuse at the front desk. After the relaxing massage, the masseuse handed me another letter as she wished me a happy birthday before I exited. This letter read, "I hoped, you enjoyed your massage but that's not all. There's something for you at the restaurant we had our very first date." It was a no-brainer. The Grandview Saloon. I journeyed fifteen minutes from the East End to South Side onto Grandview Avenue in Mount Washington. When I stepped to the hostess desk, there was a short white lady with stringy brown hair in the age range of 40 to 45 standing behind.

"Welcome to Grandview Saloon. How many people?" She said.

"It's just me. My girlfriend got me on a scavenger hunt. This is one of the places she told me to come." While I'm speaking, the hostess reached under the desk. She handed me a white envelope.

"Oh, here you go. You must be the special birthday boy. She dropped this off yesterday." I got a table and order tacos for a late lunch. When opening the third card; two tickets dropped out onto the table. When I flipped the tickets over. I read with big eyes, almost falling out of my seat. Drake & Future- Summer Sixteen concert tickets. Future until this day is my favorite rapper after the Jay-Z, Biggie, Outcast, UGK, Jeezy, and Project Pat. It was one of the best concerts I experienced in my adult life.

As time went by, we celebrated the holidays. Dressed as Black Panthers on Halloween, split time; eating at both parent's houses on Thanksgiving, danced and made cookies with the kids on Christmas Eve, open gifts on Christmas Day, and counted down numbers in the cold January night downtown Pittsburgh to kiss at 0 on New Year's Day.

On Valentine's Day, I hired Ebony Murray with Cluttered Design to decorate the hair salon. At the entrance, there was an arch of balloons in red, pink, purple, and clear. Balloons were scattered on the floor as an accessory to the rose pedals. On the countertop in the waiting room, I placed a huge stuffy brown teddy bear and a hundred roses beside one other. I was not there to witness the expression on Britany's face. When she called via Facetime she was overly delighted.

The next morning after our Valentine dinner the night before she all of a sudden got out the bed.

"I'll be back." Were the only words, she spoke as she got dressed then flew wherever. My consciousness knew she was on her way to the store to purchase a Plan B which she has bought once before in the early stage of the relationship or a pregnancy test. When she came back into the house, she hurried into the bathroom. As she passed I heard a plastic bag shake, then the door slam, the toilet shut then a sound of piss drizzling down in the water. In the interior of three minutes behind the closed door of the bathroom she wailed

"Oh no, Oh my God. Oh, my God no!"

I rushed out the bed, took two steps towards the bathroom then stood outside the door.

"Everything okay," I asked with a slight bit of concern. The door swung slow, she was sitting on the toilet looking like someone had flushed her happiness away.

"I'm pregnant." She handed me the pregnancy test. I observed and seen the line that showed positive. At that moment, I had mixed feelings. I was ecstatic but at the same, all I could think of is being a father to four kids. We agreed to keep our child. I'm so grateful we did. I'm grateful for all four despite the shit I went through with some of the mothers.

Before and during the pregnancy we traveled. The cool vibe and dirty streets of Los Angeles, California, the desert blazing hot city of Scottsdale, Arizona, and even The Grand Canyon at the National Park. The Sight of the colorful deep Canyon was definitely beyond breathtaking and did not seem real. It blows my mind how a set of rocks appear 3D to the eyes, pictures in the social sciences books in grade school can't compare. We went to Philadelphia and a few other cities. Though we didn't travel out of the states this was a huge wake-up call for me. Before Britany I was one of those individuals who never thought of exploring past the mountains of Pittsburgh. My mindset was Pittsburgh. I was glued to the bottoms of the city. I bet there's a ton of people in their own city that haven't crossed state lines. If you don't get anything out of this chapter get this. There is more to experience in this big world other than just your city. The money you spend at a bar or a club every weekend could go towards a plane ticket and a place to lay your head. After the breakup with Britany and as soon, as I'd got over my depression I said fuck it then traveled like a mothafuck.

I've been culture-struck by all the Black People in Atlanta and the DMV. It wasn't just Black People it was the successful black people that surprised me. I hit Houston, New Orleans, North Carolinas, New York, back to LA, two-hour road trips to Cleveland and a few others cities. One fact considering Ohio that people don't know. Ohio has some of the most beautiful women in the country and they're some bona fide freaks.

April of 2017 I moved out of the apartment in Turtle Creek Pa and then Britany and I moved to a six-bedroom house in Swissvale Pa. She no longer was under the wings of her parents' inherited house. She now was free. Britany was able to live how she desired in her own comfort without pressure. The season of spring and summer flew past quickly. When fall came upon we had our healthy bundle of joy. A month after our child, on November 3rd I proposed outside in front of her hair salon.

When 2018 came in to play in January, my homeboy Carlos told me that I was built like a grizzly bear. He was right, on the scale I weighed 214 pounds. My stomach stuck out like a sore thumb and I had bulging embarrassing man boobs, especially when I wore white t-shirts. I had bad indigestion and any foods I ate would burn a hole in my throat. Britany was a nutritious coach. I've seen her weight loss results in the past using the Herbalife Supplements. I drank the shakes and tea momentarily but I never considered taking it seriously. Britany gave me a guide to follow to lose weight. Hot Herbalife tea in the morning to speed the metabolism, which burned up to 300 calories. Two Herbalife healthy meal protein shakes a day and a colorful meal. **Example:** *baked chicken or fish, sweet potatoes, and a green vegetable.* After the pregnancy, she became plump from the baby weight. So, we both decided to go on this losing weight journey together. We followed the plan, alternated times to watch our child so one can get time in the gym, we worked out at the park and in the comfort of our home. Within five months on a strict plan, she lost 25 pounds and became tone in all the right places. I dropped from 214 down to 165 and I became more positive in the process along with having more energy to battle the life obstacles. When you build your stamina in the gym and eat healthy foods, your sex game will increase to its peak. You will last longer and be less fatigued. That's for both sexes.

While losing weight, we were beyond the limits of busy. I had published the second book, quit my stressful job, bought a cargo van, got a contract delivering narcotics, and began a carpet cleaning business. She was in the salon with a stacked book from noon to 10pm sometimes later than that. On top of our busy lifestyle, we had a mobile infant and no time for one another. She would come home drained mentally. Being a psychologist, a friend, and listening to clients and her employee's adversities, operating a smooth business, coloring, and styling hair combined with being a boss put a load on her shoulders.

There were days she placed her frustrations on me. Especially at the beginning of my leap of faith by quitting my job and exploring to be an entrepreneur. The money was coming in turtle slow. I would get one or two carpet-cleaning clients a week and the first contract; I cashed in $150 - $200 a week. So, I understood her frustration but at the same time, I was not ready for her to bring that boss mood into the house.

Every man wants a powerful gorgeous black queen until he begins to date one. Then they come to the realization that he has to step his own shit up. As time went by and the word spread considering my carpet business I began to get more clients, then I landed a delivery contract paying $900 a week. As I stacked clients, our relationship began to fall apart bit by bit.

This one client came to the door with shiny chocolate skin, oiled down from head to toes just wearing a bra and panties. It made it no better than she was a very attractive woman. If it was the young Tink. He would've entered the apartment while the lady's body was exposed. Wait for flirtatious signals, say some slick player shit then possibly fuck her on the couch of the living room. Instead, I kindly told the lady that I can't clean her carpets unless she was fully dressed. She apologized saying sorry and mentioning she just got out of the shower. She told me to wait. Glaring through the clear screen door all I surveyed was a phat round buttered up cocoa booty switching up the stairway. All I could do is scratch my head and not allow temptation to get the best of me. *I ended up with this woman at the beginning of the pandemic.*

I told my best friend Wade and Roland, Britany's friend's husband that I was close to at the time regarding the woman that came to the door half-naked. Britany asked if a woman tried to push up on me while cleaning carpets multiple times. I flat-out told her no. simple as that. A month later, she asked the same question. I flat-out told her no again. I could've voiced to her about the woman coming to the door half-naked but I choose not to. She beforehand had trust issues. I couldn't like women's photos on social media; I would get accused of looking at random women standing near us. The worst is when I began to notice unread messages being read in my directed messages on Instagram. It went as far as Britany arguing through the messages with women I would never think of talking to even if I was a horny single man. I was trying to protect her security and freedom from anxiety each time I went to clean a client's carpet. Not telling her the truth spiked her insecurity when she already knew the truth. Roland has told his wife and it watered down to Britany. Shit got even worst when I changed the password on all social media platforms. She was checking my phone or the mac book more often than usual.
This one day I sent Wade a screenshot of this woman we grew up with. This individual had a major crush on me through high school up to my early 20's. Back then, she was not that appealing to me. Now her glow was bright. I wrote under the photo the text read.

"I should've fucked her back then. She's bad now."

Word of advice to you men who wants to be sneaky. Your messages between you and your boys will get you in trouble. Delete that shit. Our relationship was falling and the trust she had for me was decreasing week by week.

Weeks later while we both relaxed on the couch. She has just got off work it's about 11pm. My phone was on the charger beside her when a random call from a 504- New Orleans number was displayed on the screen. Britany hurried and answer on speaker.

"Hello." The deep New Orleans voice butterflied. It was Lamara the woman from New Orleans who taught me how to give pleasure to women. I had my phone number since high school I would get random calls all the time. The next day she gave me the ultimatum to change the number that I was attached to or she would leave the relationship. She sat her ring on the counter and I had to choose as she walked out the door to head to work. The last thing I wanted was to lose my family over a phone number so I changed it. When I did I delivered roses and lunch to the salon while she was styling someone's hair.

"I changed the number." The expression on her face showed more excitement than me presenting the engagement ring. Tears flowed down her face as she hugged me with all emotions releasing through.

January - May 2019

Our relationship was up and down like a yoyo. Some weeks were perfect the other weeks we couldn't stand each other. We went to counseling to give us balance. Though they were a married couple, who counseled for a living through the word of God I did not think it was the best idea to be counsel church friends. It seemed like the weight was all on me. It was three against one.

A time during counseling, she poured all her feelings on the table. It was messy. First, I learned that she knew all this time about the woman coming to the door half-naked. Wade and

Roland were the exclusive people who knew in regards to the woman coming to the door. I surely knew Wade didn't break the man code. Roland was the definite suspect but I was in denial. I remained good friends with him at the time because I was not sure. She went on saying she fell in love with the person I once was. I considered her feelings. I would fix everything else but not our relationship, she mentioned that I haven't plan dates in a while. Then she went on about me writing erotic books saying she wanted me to write a different genre. In the final analysis, she spoke on the text between Wade and I and me changing the password to all my social media.

It was my turn to speak.

"I don't think neither one of us are the same people as we were at the beginning. I feel like I'm in this relationship alone. I think you're insecure."
"Don't call me insecure." She said.

"You repeatedly bring up the past. We'll be having a decent day then you'll bring up an old argument. I changed my number for you and did whatever it takes to keep you here."

She interrupted again. "I had to threaten you. You should've changed your number when you proposed to me"

"Can I talk," I said with squinted eyes while shaking my head. And one thing I'm not doing is changing my writing genre. You just complain about everything. I'm just tired of it."

Some of the words she laid on the table were true. As we began to grow apart, I became selfish and put everything else before putting the queen on the pedestal. The less attention I got I sought it elsewhere. The weight loss had me feeling myself more. I was drowning in my own ego. I let pride get in the way, which lead to a break-up letter.

The end of the letter.

"I have to cut ties with you, Darren. (As I cry saying this) but it's true. I have to let you go because you don't value me like I want to be valued. I love you with every ounce in my body!"

Three days later after reading the break-up letter Britany the ex-fiancé pointed the gun at me in the middle of the stairwell while I stood in the center of the living room not as afraid as I should've been. She was in a rage because a woman texted my phone saying she missed me.

Knock, knock, knock, knock at the front door. I crept to the door to open as the gun pointing followed me.

"It's Roland and Taja. Immediately I opened the door then the couple split us apart and brought Britany back to her senses.

Never let pride get in the way. You will lose everything. The better man always listens to his woman's needs. Ignoring them will make shit worst. A year later Britany got married to another man. I'm going to close this chapter out like this. The woman one man doesn't appreciate another will.

012. Newly Dating

2019 July- 2021

After I got over my depression, following the breakup with my ex-fiancée. I was placed back on the market. I took the time to figure myself out before I began to talk to anyone else. During this dating, messing around, and talking process I recognized a ton of shit that I was blinded to in my younger life. Now that I was more mature, I could see past the pleasure of just getting pussy.

Summer of 2019

I met this beautiful popular Instagram woman in a bar on East Carson Street in Pittsburgh. Every photo she posted on social media was highly flooded with hearts from other Insta users. Everything from the location of the photos to the stylish clothes she wore was exquisite. That night before speaking to Stacy I observed every mother's son gazing at this woman. She was a catch to the eyes. I have to admit I caught myself peeking too. Stacy was a yellow bone with natural black curly hair; she looked like she was an exotic island woman from Hawaii. All that she needed was a flower in the right ear.

Fun fact: a flower behind the left ear states that you're married or you're not for the streets. A flower in the right ear means you're single and you are for the streets.

The tight nude dress hugging her thick behind had men crowded around the woman and her friends. I moved around throughout the busy bar and paid Stacy no mind. There were too many women in the place to be stuck on one. While all the birds went after the one piece of bread, I spread my wings to find a loaf.

Later in the night, moving through the crowded bar I passed Stacy and her heavyset friend who was also a yellow bone with a big forehead. She was an attractive woman. The friend stopped me as I attempted to slide past her.

"Mmmm, you smell good." She said, slurring her words as she leaning towards me.
"Thank you," I smirked as she sniffed me.
"Mmmm what is that?" she asked. Before I could answer, Stacy stood up
"Can I smell," she questioned leaning towards me to get a sniff.
"You do smell good." She said, then stepped back to get a full view of me. Then she continued.
"And he's cute too."
"I know, right." The heavier woman followed up.

"Thank you, both" I replied nonchalantly. Too much was going on in the bar. People were moving through the bar shoulder to shoulder attempting to slide past. To skip all the small talk, I pulled the phone out.

"Hey, let's get a bite someday, what's your number." Just like that, she dialed her number on my phone.

Take care. Free game for the men.

Cologne is the worm on the hook of a fishing rod. It's bait to seize the swimming fishes. Recently when I visited Atlanta, I went to Café Circa A Lounge on Edgewood Avenue. On the second floor of the lounge, there was an open roof bar. It was easier to order food and drinks downstairs. After deciding not to order, I made my way back to the rooftop where the party was jumping. As I was going up the steps, a group of women was coming down. When I reached the top, I heard two or three voices

"He smells good." When I glanced back to say "Thank you." Four girls stampeded up the steps. Four women were in my face visiting from Detroit staring me down like they were waiting to be picked up on the narrow steps. I could've done eeny, meeny, miny, moe. Instead, I gave them all my Instagram and told them to buy my next book.

Women love a man who takes care of himself. Smelling good will have a woman fall for you before any designer clothing, manicure, pedicure, white teeth, or wearing nice underwear and socks. Finally, yet importantly a man that can dress. Invest in yourself. Buy the more expensive toothpaste and toothbrush, the high-end cologne, get haircuts, and eat healthy.

Back to the story

After a week of texting, I took Stacy to Doce Taqueria. I took most women to this taco spot for a first date. When a woman gets past the first date, I would take the woman to a better place to eat. In the past year, two individuals advanced to second dates, there could've been a third but she disappeared after the first date. At this time, I was a serial dater. Stacy had a big personality and she was unquestionably outgoing. Everybody loved Stacy, from the lady taking the orders, to the man outside walking the dog. She spoke and laughed with everyone. The same night she had to be home by a certain time to release her child from the family babysitter. She lived close by these projects in the cut on the South Side. In front of Stacy's apartment, we relaxed in my carpet cleaning van and shared words for a second. Then the next minute we were touching all on each other under the orange streetlights. Soon as she positioned herself to suck my dick, Stacy's phone rang and she answered it on speaker.
"Hey, mom,"
"Hey, when will you be here?"

"I'm outside right now. Give me a few seconds."

"I would stay longer Stac I just have to be at work at 6 am."

"Okay. Give me a second." Stacy repeated, and then hung up. Then she grasped my hard-black manhood which was hanging out the zipper. Awkwardly she kneeled in the empty gap between the driver and passenger seat of the cargo van. Stacy licked the length of my penis from the root to the head. She was buttering me up like corn on the cob licking all sides of my shaft. Soon after she sealed her mouth over me and then began to suck slowly as she stroked with her right hand in the same motion of her face bobbing. I felt my toes curling in my dirty work shoes as I relaxed while a small handful of vehicles rode past in the night with their headlights beaming. Nas said it the best "Females who are the sexiest are always the nastiest." She was taking me in deep down in her throat. Mid-facial Stacy's phone rang again. She lifted her head up and answered with frustration in her tone as shiny saliva leaked down her chin.

"I'm coming." Then hung up.

"My mom wants to get home to her boyfriend that all. What are you doing in the next hour or two?"

"I'm going home when I leave here. Why what's up."

"When I put the baby to sleep. You can come back."

"I have to work in the morning. The only way I'll come in is if I stay." I said.

"That's fine, I'll text you when he's in bed." When she stepped out of the van, I respectfully waited until she got into the house first before pulling off.

I received the text within an hour and forty-five minutes. I had taken a shower and packed an overnight bag with clothes, a toothbrush, and a box of three condoms. I was overjoyed; this was some pussy a lot of men wished they could fuck. Then again, I would never know what type of woman she was because I barely knew her. She could've been out here fucking all avatars of men. What should I expect this was our first date? It ended with a result of me been invited. Maybe she was feeling me so naturally that she felt comfortable for me to step into her world of peace.

When I parked then stepped out of the van an all-black, tinted vehicle with the trunk-rattling through the music bass blasting as the car passed by sluggishly. I held my breath for a half minute as my heart raced like a 100-meter track runner. My gun was deep under the seat. If some shit was to go down I would be fried like a Thanksgiving turkey. Once fear shaded off my bones I walked up the steep steps. Once I stepped on the porch, I noticed a mountain of filled white garbage in the corner of the porch. It had to be at least fifteen bags of trash. Some bags were ripped in the middle with trash easing out. Droplets of food, scattered pop cans, and the bottom of the meat package laid on the ground. I became more paranoid on the porch than I was when the black car crept down the street. I was on high alert for any kinds of rodents or animals playing Jack in the Box on the porch. I texted. "Come to the door," before going up the step.

"Okay. She replied. I figured in the time I came up the steps the door should be swinging open. On the other hand, I stood tense, being patient as possible for one minute; scoping the outside scenery as I listened to the cricket's chip. Once the 60 seconds were expired I texted
"I'm outside." Then immediately after that, I called. She answered at the first ring.
"I'm at the door.
"I'm sorry here I come." She said. Stacy sounded like she was in the middle of moving around.

When she answered the door, she gave me a loving hug. This was when the story made a devastating turn. This I when I learned that social media was deceiving and hollow. Coming through the entrance Stacy had an 80inch flat-screen

TV sitting on a mix of orange and black milk crates. She had no sofa or love seat. There were three folding outdoor lounger chairs with a full bowl of ramen noodles and an open bag of Cool Ranch Doritos beside the middle chair. Unexplainable trash lay on the floor. In the far corner to the left; a table lamp with no lampshade on the floor. As I follow Stacy through the living room, my shoes barely pulled from the grimy sat on the carpet. If I stepped fast enough my foot would probably lift out the shoe. The carpet was coated with black gooey shit; dust mites, crumbs, and all types of allergens covered the fibers.

The apartment smelled like fresh dryer sheets. I heard a machine in motion as she guided me upstairs, the stairway was used as a shoe rack. When strolling through the hall there was a trail of trash, clothes, and unrolled toilet paper all over the floor.

"Excuse the mess." She said kicking an empty Minute Maid orange juice carton to the side. When she opened the door to the bedroom, I was floored; just like the mattress with no sheets over top. I did not want to sit my bag down let alone sit in the bed.

"Where's your bathroom at?" I asked. As she flopped onto the twin mattress with her phone in hand.

"The bathroom is right across the hall." She said then turned her attention to the phone. I carried the bag with me to the disgusting bathroom. There was an overpowering aroma of dark yellow piss in the toilet; toothpaste splattered all over the window, rubbished filled to the brim of the garbage can and a black ring circled the tub.

I could get in contact with neither of my homie to save me with an exit call. So instead I told the complete truth soon as I stepped foot back in the room.

"It would've been nice to stay with you tonight. I'm not feeling the way you live." I explained everything from the grimy carpets to the ring in the tub."

"Something mothers have to deal with."

"I agree but not tonight maybe another time." I understood that a kid would leave a house junky but there was a big difference in filthy. When I went home I tried to get on her page but couldn't because I was blocked.

Fall Date 2019

I broke the first taco date rule for a fine chocolate petite woman. We went to Duke's in Homestead, PA where there's a bar and delicious bar food. When Davida and I received our food, she appeared scared to eat in front of me. She would nibble on the tenders then wipe her mouth or take a tiny bite of a French Fry. When I glanced at the television she would take a rapid bite then hold the food in her mouth and chewed slowly when I turned my view towards her.

This was more than annoying, I would rather a woman devour her meal and eat the way she normally did when she was alone. I wanted to see a woman dig into her food with sauce on the lips and enjoy whatever was ordered on the menu. My mother told me a while ago, a woman who was afraid to eat in front of a man was insecure. This was our first and last night I was not feeling that woman's unhinged spirit.

March of 2020

Stormy, 23 years old

I named her stormy because of the gray lace wig and the sarcastic smart mouth she carried. If there were a third member of the City Girls she would be the one. From the way her body was built to the belly shirt and the booty shorts, the extra-long colorful gripper nails, to the extended eyelashes and saying "period" at the end of almost every sentence, she fit the mold. Stormy would fit in just right with the rap group.

Stormy was entertaining to be around, we actually had fun and turned up together numerous times. My dilemma with Stormy was she did not know when to sit her ass down when it was time. She expected me to be toxic and match her negative energy. On occasions, she would attempt to undertake an argument. She would type long-ass text messages, two-minute voice mails, or in-person utter a million words in one breath that didn't make sense to me. Each word went out one ear and out the other. Since the beginning of being a single man and after the long relationship, I was over the arguing stage. You would have to push my button over the max to get me upset to argue with anyone.

The sexual connection between us aligned perfectly. We were both Leos with an exceedingly high sex drive. When we fucked it was like two jungle cats fighting. She would scratch, punch and bite while I would choke her throat firmly, send power strokes to charge her soul, aggressively flipped every and which way, and slap handprints on her golden ass. There was not one time I would survive. I would always come out the pussy with a war wound. Sometimes I had deep digging scratch marks on my back and neck, a busted lip, or a sore arm.

Stormy was obsessed with the Onlyfans site. She would mention to me with a serious expression "This my business. I cashed in $300 today. Period!" She went on. "Babe, say period."

She began an Onlyfans page two months before we became friends. The page consisted of videos of Stormy dancing naked, shower videos with soap cascading down her ass, and videos with her legs spread as she stimulated her clit. Stormy requested me to be a guest in the Onlyfans format. She hasn't had anyone else but herself on the page. So, I agreed. Upon terms that my face was left out the video. Stormy slobbed me down viciously as I held the camera to shoot with perfection until I squirted a load in Stormy's open mouth. We made several more videos of me getting head and a single video of me blindfolded devouring her pussy. Stormy was banking making up to $6,000 in a month. I did not get one dime and did not care to. She bought a car then moved into a new apartment.

Around this time, I had an abundance of women. Two women in Cleveland, Ohio; both owned successful boutique stores. This fine thick healthy cocoa woman in Baltimore, Maryland who had to repeat almost every word when she spoke because I couldn't understand her accent. A sweet pretty, big forehead woman in Akron, Ohio who loved the ground that I walked on and I never gave a fair chance to. I maintained an excuse for why we couldn't be together while other men would beg for her attention. A dread head woman who taught me that the source of energy was within myself. She was into crystals, rocks, stones, and beads. She performed reiki on me. I believe until this day I levitated over the table. I still use sage and incense because of her.

There was also an Asian woman who named me BDDD Big Dick Daddy Darren. She texted when she wanted to fuck and she loved to drink the cum out of me. She would remind me all the time that I tasted sweet. That was because I consumed a smoothie full of berries every morning. When I penetrated the Asian woman from behind. I admired her fully colorful tatted back with Japanese words, symbols, and dragons. She was fascinated with my chocolate melanin. She would say, "you're so chocolate."

Then there was Sky a woman I met in the grocery store. She bragged via FaceTime to her friend about me in the bed considering how intense and amazing the dick was explaining details to said friend. Weeks later, the same was laying in the same spot Sky slept.

A lot of women say, "My friends would never." It may be true but you still planted that seed in your friend's mind that the man you were dating had something pleasant hanging down his thighs. She may not have known at the time you and the guy were dealing with one another. If you and the guy fall off some way, your friend may be the first woman on his heels to fill your shoes since you planted the seed in the first place. Some shit you just have to keep reserved for yourself. There were so many more women, a teacher, flight attendant, hairstylist, bartender, dancer, and a gym junkie. I was buying boxes of condoms like chain smokers bought cigarettes. I was drowning myself in women and juggling souls.

On a Sunday night of September 2019, I was passing by the McKees Rocks Bridge. I saw two ladies standing beside a car with their blinkers flashing. I sought out to do at least one good deed a day. This was my opportunity to assist someone. So, instead of riding past and minding my business, I pulled over. When I stepped out, I noticed a deflated tire on the passenger rear side and a donut tire resting on the side. Then I noticed two men circling the vehicle as I approached the ladies.

"Hey, everything okay. I see y'all have a flat." The men stepped closer as I spoke to the ladies.

"Yes. We're waiting for a tow truck to come change the tire." The thick yellow bone with short hair announced.

"I'm sorry. Let me introduce myself. I'm Tinker or Tink for short." I allowed my eyes to scan everyone. One of the guys stopped brushing his hair to shake my hand and the other guy followed after. Both stating their names. Shortly after the men, the women submitted their names as well. Courtney was perfectly thick, skin tone the color of graham crackers, her hair was styled short and brown with blonde highlights. Toria had milk chocolate skin, she was slims with a slight bit of thickness. She wore lengthy braids that ended near the tailbone. Toria was chewing the fuck out of gum with frustration written all over her face.

"What's the estimated time that the tow truck will be here?"The guy brushing his hair spoke before everyone else could.

"An hour up to two."

"Why don't ya'll just change to the donut now? Then get a tire tomorrow."
Toria burst out blowing steam. She must have been the driver.
"These ni**as don't know how to change a tire!" She smacked the chewing gum. Both men could not say a word. Homeboy brushed his hair while the other guy went back to wherever he was before I stepped in the picture.

"I'm not trying hear this shit." He mumbled under his breath.
"I'll change it. Where's the jack that come with the car."

In the aftermath of getting my hands, dirty Toria slipped me a balled-up piece of paper. Before revealing what was written inside in the wrinkles of the receipt, I had no idea it was her number. What happened was their men could not recuse them out of something simple as changing a donut. The men weren't dependable and were beyond worthless. I was certain Toria and Courtney lost all respect for their boyfriends that day. They wanted to be safe and kept out of danger. This night I became their hero, their knight shining armor while clowns watched in the background.

Two weekends later, the two were at the hotel suite I had booked for a get-together I had a day before. One of my homeboys was supposed to be on his way to meet Courtney. I was calling this man phone back to back. He was not answering after I talked to him forty minutes earlier. After the fifth game of Uno Toria spoke up. "I'm bored."

"Me too. Where is your boy?" Courtney asked. I tried to entertain the women the best I could. The music, drinks, and the game of Uno would not cut it.

"I honestly don't know. He's not answering. What ya'll want to do?"

"I don't know." They said in unison.

"Okay. Let's ask each other sex questions, if you don't answer you have to take a shot."
"Sex questions like what?" Toria asked.
"Anything sexually-that comes to your mind that you want to ask."
"I'm the third wheel," Courtney uttered.
"So what bitch, you're playing. I know all your secrets." Toria said in a joking matter.
"You first Courtney. Ask anyone a question." I said

"Ahhh." She shifted her eyes at Toria and I scanned to pick then she continued. "Toria, how many dicks you sucked in your life?"

"Five." She giggled.

"Bitch you're lying take a shot." Courtney laughed. After a couple of rounds of questions, one question changed the game.

"Courtney, have you ever watched your friend get her pussy ate." We were drinking and I went for it.

"No. we never did nothing in front of each other," Courtney answered specifically.

"If I ate your friend's pussy now, would you watch?" I asked.
        "What? Eat my pussy? You want to eat my pussy?" Toria sound surprised.

        "Yes. Only if Courtney watched."

Toria glance at her friend. "This crazy. I'm down if she is." Toria said.

        "Okay, I'll watch."

        The ladies were sitting on the couch diagonal to where I sat. Toria whispered in Courtney's ear for a split second.

        "We'll be right back, where's the bathroom?"

        The ladies disappeared in the bathroom for no longer than five minutes. I wish I were a fly on the wall. I would be tuned into the conversation they engaged in behind closed doors. Whatever they talked about the girls came out the bathroom giggly before flopping on the couch. All while they were in the restroom I took a shot, poured them both a shot, another one for myself, and then I dimmed the lights low in the living room suite.

"Let's toast to a good time tonight," I said, sitting on the coffee table about a foot across the ladies.

"To a good time." We said in unison.

We all raised our shot glasses, tapped glasses then took back the alcohol in one swallow.
"I'm about to change your life." I manifested, speaking to Toria as I positioned myself upon the floor in between her legs. Toria had a humongous smile on her face as she shot her attention to Courtney crawling to the corner of the couch, smiling as well.

"Oh my gosh, I can't believe I'm allowing you to do this." She voiced as reality struck. In no time, I was unfastening her tight distressed blue jeans. I struggled for a second to slide her pants off she assisted by lifting her waist upward from the couch to make it easier. Her entire left thigh was tatted with a dreamcatcher, roses, and some other designs. Above the tatted thighs, she wore these sexy black lace panties. Toria's pussy was bulging out the lace; it appeared like a cupcake hiding under her panties. No doubt she had a cushioned box between those thighs.

I slid her panties down her smooth legs and beautiful toes then I slowly ran my tongue up the tatted thigh. I blocked Courtney completely out for the moment. I spread the lips of Toria's pussy apart to reveal her clit. With my full tongue, I licked upwards. All smiles disappeared as I felt every nerve in Toria's body halt as she let loose her first moan. I wrapped my lips around her clit, sliding my tongue back and forth as saliva mixed with her juices streaming down my chin. Toria tasted crisp like water with cucumbers inside.

"Oh my gosh! Yes!" She wailed while my tongue wrote an erotic story in love box. "Yes! Yes! Right there."

She continued. In my peripheral, Courtney seemed unstable on the corner of the couch. She kept adjusting herself on the couch as she watched without blinking. I devoured Toria as she got ready for a third climax. My right hand fished around for Courtney. The second I got a grasped hold of Courtney's thigh I skimmed my hand up to the crotch of her sweatpants. I brushed my fingers upon her pussy. Her warm juices were seeping out of the fabric. I lifted my face out of Toria's water like a swimmer coming up for air.

"Take those pants off," I demanded then buried my face back into the pool of Toria. My lips were massaging the outside while my tongue was stimulating the clit. I felt a ton of movement on the right side. When the movement decreased, my hand fished once more to grasp a handful of thick thighs without fabric over the surface. Courtney scooted beside her friend. Right away, I plugged my index and middle fingers inside of Courtney's overflowing wetness. My palm faced upward, fingers curled, fingertips sweeping the sponge ceiling of Courtney's box.

"I'm cumin. I'm cumin." Toria announced as Courtney wailed each and every time I plunged my fingers in her.

Toria's hands clenched on the back of my head. "Oh my gosh, oh my gosh, oh my gosh!" Hearing both of the women take possession of pleasure made me feel powerful. Like I was the mothafuckin man.

Soon as Toria climaxed, I crossed over to eat Courtney's passion fruit. She flowed slippery, tasted sweet and the texture of her love button was tender. As I fed on Courtney. Toria hovered over her friend then began dropping soft kisses onto Courtney's chest. Then the next minute they were tonguing each other down, trading saliva. Tongue kissing sent a signal to the vagina, which I mentioned, in one of the past chapters. With Toria slobbing Courtney and myself stimulating the clit by sucking and licking. Courtney was at her highest peak; I felt her legs vibrating and observed her stomach sinking in and out. I just kept licking, licking, licking, and licking then she erupted screaming and pouring out pleasure onto my beard.

"Let's go in the bedroom," I said wiping the cum dripping off the tip of the hairs on my beard.

The ladies followed my lead into the dark room, the single light that shined was coming from behind the cracked bathroom door. The ladies climbed on the bed at the same time that I took off my clothes. Without me in the mix, they were in the middle of the mattress fully naked all over one another. Even though I had plenty of threesomes. It still amazed me to watch two women intertwined. *To be truthful. More straight women watch lesbian flicks than straight porn.* They touched one another with so much natural passion that a man may take years to perfect. I stood at the foot end of the bed taking in the scenery as I stroked my hard-black shaft. They were so into the moment I placed my hormones to the side and allow them to play.

Toria got a peep of lonely me standing like an anxious pup. She whispered in Courtney's ear. The next second I know they glared at me like beautiful hungry wolves craving for meat as they came towards me. Courtney covered her mouth over my hardness then began sucking as Toria planted kisses on my neck. I grasped Toria's throat and then slid my tongue down her tonsils. Courtney spat on my manhood right after she stroked every length of this chocolate pole. After the spit-shined, she threw her neck in repeatedly, slurping and drooling all over the bedsheets. Soon as I released Toria from my grasp, she lowered her face to Courtney's level. Courtney immediately passed the microphone to Toria. Toria sang solo for a second then Courtney joined in for a duet. I stood with weak knees like noodles in hot water as I held both heads in my palms. Courtney sank lower and gently painted her tongue across my genitals in the time Toria continue to please orally.

Before I was able to cum I put the oral to a halt, any minute longer I would've been shooting clear fluids in the faces of the ladies. I mounted myself up on the bed. Sitting up straight on my knees, I clinch both ladies by the throats and then pulled them in close to me. Tonguing down one by one, then all together we dangled our love language. In the middle of kissing one of their hands was stroking my tube.

For a fact Toria was originally my company and Courtney was supposed to be for my no-show friend. In advance, I knew when It comes to laying the dick down Toria was the first.

"Toria lay down."
"No, I want to taste her," Courtney announced.

Toria glared at her friend with an open mouth dumbfounded. The expression of confusion was scribbled over her face.

"Good, Courtney you bring your ass here, and you sit on her face." I pulled Courtney toward me, placed her legs over my shoulder then gradually filled her up with hard D. I felt her body tighten up while I sent soft strokes. Toria all of a sudden seemed nervous. I assume this was her first time allowing a woman to actually touch in a such way. Courtney, she had been there done that. I could tell by the way she pulled her friend's leg

"Come here." She said in moans. Toria towered over the top of Courtney's face, her body facing towards mines. Courtney clinched her hands over Toria's ass full of graceful stretch marks then she went to business on her playmate as I faithfully laid dick between her thick thighs. As I'm penetrating Courtney, my tongue was tangling with Toria, both women were wailing with pleasuring.

Later the position was switched, this time I was throwing manhood in Toria in a doggy style angle as Courtney held Toria's head down between her legs.

"Yes, eat that pussy. Yes, best friend, yes." I took a look at the ceiling as the room filled with so much passion. "Mum, damn. Damn." I couldn't hold my moans while I delivered consistent strokes in Toria's tight box.

Toria lifted her face from Courtney's bowl of water "Yes, yes right there." She communicated. Then she went on speaking word for word.
"I'mma. About. To. Cum." Courtney hyped her friend as she played with her own pussy.

"Cum for daddy, cum for daddy." Courtney cheered. In no time, Toria's body went into an insane shock, she trembled forward screaming from the top of her lungs. Soon as I pulled my dick out of Toria, Courtney crawled towards me to taste the essence of her friend. Courtney began to throw her face at me, then Toria joined soon after she was back in one piece.

As time went on, Courtney rode me like a bull as I slurped and slithered my tongue against Toria's clit while she sat on my handsomeness. The time I came is when Toria was laid on her back in a missionary position. Courtney was sucking Toria's Pretty toes at the same time. I hurried then pulled out; pulling off the fifth condom had, then shot a hot heavy load all over Toria's stomach. We all went to sleep, then in the morning, we were back at it. Toria and I talk for a month or so but we did not get far. After all, she still had a boyfriend.

013. The Realization

Believe it or not, when you are committed and loyal to a woman, blessings will pour in abundantly. Especially when you have a woman who supports your dreams, who you have an undeniable connection with, and someone who eventually sounds like your mother because she gives a fuck and wants to watch her man elevate. Fellas if you have a diamond, don't pick a shiny rock out of the gravel because it looks good. That shiny rock you picked up might not have the value of the diamond you already had. You don't want to lose your diamond. Giving that they're hard to find in gravel surround by dirt, stones, mud, and rocks. Good women now of days in this social media era are hard to find. It's probably the same for women as well.

Many of times I've seen men with a significant number of beautiful women get worn to a frazzled then desperately date someone they normally wouldn't.

They'll have all the candy they could imagine in the sweets store, then settle on a rotten banana or become a lonely man.

Bitchassness

Dealing with hundreds of women in my early life; there's a heap of shit I'd done that I'm not proud of. The past four years had changed my mindset, my heart, and the way I approached situations. With growth, you have to acknowledge your demons, your wrongdoings, and the mental damage you caused to others. In my grown stage, I did not argue with women. I was firm with how I felt and what I believed. I was always open to listen but when I tell a woman my thoughts once that is that. She could curse a million words. I would remain calm and would not let anyone, in general, bring me out of my higher place. There were times I would slightly slip then in a split second I would catch myself.

Arguing, screaming, calling a woman out of her name will have a woman lose respect for the man. Screaming from the top of your lungs, getting beyond emotional made any man come off as a bitch. Slamming doors, throwing shit, damaging a woman's property, or mentioning something that would drop her self-esteem will also put you in the bitch category.

In my 20's I had a stretch of bitch ass ways. A woman I was dating had three kids, we got into a shootout. Long before our argument, she trusted me enough to share her dark secrets. As we were in a shouting match in the kitchen, I brought up her unfortunate past dilemmas.

"No one will never be with you; you're getting fat and you don't know who your baby father is. you're a whore." I mentally abused her. When those hurtful words left my mouth, they stung. I witnessed the woman's heart fall out of her chest as she melted to the floor with her back to the washing machine while she cried crocodile tears in a ball. I felt like shit after that moment. No matter how upset a man gets it's never right to put a woman at her lowest. A man should uplift his woman at all times. I should've said what was on my mind. If she remained heated I should've just walked away, took a ride, or found a separate room from the bullshit. You may say it was running away from the situation but sometimes it's not. If you can't talk to me like a human with respect then we can't converse.

Another bitchassness: If a man has to talk down on his woman, he is currently with to another woman to attempt to get some pussy that is a humongous no-no. If you going to cheat, just cheat. No need to throw your woman's dirty laundry at the woman you hardly know or someone that has deep feelings for you. You don't want the mistress to have two up on your woman. Cheating is one up. If you and the lady you decided to sleep with fell out, every piece of info you shared would eventually circle back to your woman. This would cause your woman to be embarrassed and make her look dumb as shit. Not all but some women can get over the cheating. When you air a woman's personal business out there's no coming back from that.

I would never ask a woman to drop her hoes for me. That's signs of a bitchassness. If a woman felt like you were applying consistent pressure and she knew for sure you're serious, she would eventually cut off the thousand men who text "good morning" in the am the man who text "wyd" every night, or the man she talks to once or twice a week. Just appreciate the time spent. If she doesn't get the memo after asking to be her man allow that woman to do her while you give others attention. One question I do not ask women. "Who else you're talking to?" It's none of my business. This is a sign of insecurity. When a woman asks this question, I'll tell them off the top I have hoes, even if I don't talk to a single soul.

There's nothing worse than an insecure man, a man who's not sure in himself. A man who's constantly assuming, searching, keeping his woman hostage from hanging with friends, or blocking his woman's blessings because he's afraid the wolves of men in the world will swallow her. As far as I'm concerned if a woman decides to risk everything for someone else, then she doesn't belong to me. she's for the streets.

2015: A serious lustful relationship

Neither one of us was faithful in the long run. At one time, I thought this woman was truly committed. As the relationship went on shit began to seem suspicious. At nights, I would search high and low through her phone while she was sleep. I found nothing and felt stupid every time. I even felt exceedingly foolish when she changed the code on her android. She used some weird app that made the alarm go off while taking a flashing selfie when the incorrect password was entered in. The next morning after the photo was taken in the middle of the night, she showed me the photo. I looked ridiculous in a dark background. All that was seen was my face with an open mouth, wide sleepy eyes filled with sneaky suspiciousness. After this moment, she did not respect me the same. She began to cheat more. The honest reason why I was searching through her phone was because of my guilty conscience.

Now of days I believe in peace and privacy. Even if a woman gives me her password, I will not waste my time out to the day to examine what she has going on in her phone. She can be a full-blown cheater if I don't know I don't know. Someday the shit she's conducting in the dark will come to the light.

Reality check

February 2021 Miami, Florida

I was in a hotel with a woman I had met at the park six months earlier. The Miami trip just felt right for me and Precious. Before coming to Florida, we haven't talked to one another in almost three weeks. The reason behind us not talking was my homie Los and I took a two-hour road trip to Cleveland, Ohio at the floods seafood lounge, Los and I watched the Steelers lose to the Browns for the first time ever. The Cleveland Browns fans were ecstatic because this was their first time making the playoffs since 2002. We were the only black and gold fans in the lounge. To celebrate our loss and their victory the group of bartenders gave us a shot to take with them. I filmed an Instagram story as we toasted with the enemies. There were four bartenders one was older somewhere in the 40s, a male, this fine chocolate woman in the mid-20s, and a gorgeous caramel complexion woman. Out of all the women on the video Precious assumed I was flirting with the caramel skin lady. She stated she was the cutie girl out of all the bartenders. Then created an entire story in her mind that did not make any sense.

One of my biggest peeves is calling me a liar. Don't call me a liar, don't make me seem like one either. Especially when I'm completely honest and there's no proof to back up the assumptions against me. In the past, she accused me several other times before the trip to Cleveland. I was annoyed with the debates and the more she pointed fingers the more I became turned off. When she called to ask if I want to come to Miami I admitted I was skeptical because being with someone for four days straight; trailing our debate I knew some shit was bound to transpire. On top of that, my funds were low after paying an attorney, a high ass fine, all my bills, and my business was dragging considering it was winter and it was the middle of a pandemic up north. So, I was dishing out a ton of money and losing out on money all in the same month. For all those reasons, I did not want to take a trip with just a thousand dollars. Two veggie hamburgers with fries and a drink may cost you two hundred dollars in Miami. She bought the plane ticket to bring the dick with her anyways. At this point that was all, I had become to someone who didn't trust a word I said. She even took a plan B pill to push her period back so we could have sex on the trip.

Saturday evening directly after we spent the entire morning and afternoon at the sunny isles beach we went back to the hotel. Her friends were at the pool on the seventh floor partying. We split ways as Precious went with her friends and I went to the room. It was Precious' birthday instead of hopping straight in the shower I googled **nearest bakeries in Miami** for the cake to be delivered for the birthday dinner. The cake was $150 I had to put a down payment down for the cake to be baked, designed, and delivered. Then there were a Whole Foods two blocks away I had planned on buying at least three dozen roses. Right after I ordered the cake, my daughter called to ask about the trip. We spoke for no longer than 10 minutes. Minutes later, I stripped to get in the shower. As soon as I gathered my clothes to take to the bathroom, the front door opened.

"You didn't get in the shower yet!" she rudely screamed. I was butt-ass naked holding clothes at the entrance of the bathroom, wonderstruck in why the hell she was yelling in such a disrespectful manner.

"No, I'm about to get in," I said calmly, then went into the spacious bathroom.

"We have to be dressed by 7, I'm getting in first! What were you doing? You probably was talking to some bitch and you sat on the bed with sand on your body." she continued as she stormed her way into the bathroom. I went from 0 to 100

"YO I SWEAR TO GOD, LEAVE ME THE FUCK ALONE!" I growled. Spit flew from my mouth as I quickly spoke. Then out of nowhere I rapidly became conscious that I was falling out of character.

"I should've never brought you here." She fired back. "We have to be downstairs at 7 and you're just sitting around bullshitting." I knew the plan was dinner that evening I did not know when the pool party was over. For a man to get dressed it takes no longer than 20 minutes. For a woman, I understand the dolled-up process took longer. I ignored her rude statement.

"You know what. I'm just going to get in this shower." I said in a harmless tone then I walked my naked ass in the shower. Peacefully the steaming hot hotel water sprayed on my face to bring me back into reality. As water cascade down my chocolate body, I came to the conclusion. If I have to get out of character with anyone then I shouldn't be dating them. When I got out of the shower she still had an attitude, throwing and slamming shit on the sink. I walked past with towel in hand to exit the bathroom. She kept mumbling words under her breath as she proceeded to throw shit around. I strolled into the bathroom with the towel around my waist.

"Since it's your birthday, I don't want to make your day any worse. I'm just going to stay here." I uttered. She did not say a word; she went about her business to get dressed.

While she scrambled around the hotel I stood outside on the balcony; taking in the Miami night breeze, glaring down from high above at the people below looking like ants and hot wheel fancy cars speeding on the busy streets. I had thoughts about how many people in Pittsburgh were in the snow with coats, sweaters, and boots meanwhile I was in Florida with shorts on and a t-shirt in the middle of February. As these thoughts registered, I heard the door slam behind me. I glanced back then went inside to scan the entire room. She was gone and the only trace of her was the flowery smell of her perfume.

Miami Solo Dolo

Sitting in the room alone scrolling through my phone on Instagram, I almost regretted that I allowed Precious to leave without me. I became dumb bored for a second, I removed my shoes then laid in the bed. I messaged a woman from New Jersey but lived in Miami. We messaged once before sharing flirtatious words back and forth in the past on social media, to be honest, she was my chocolate crush.

"Hey, I'm in Miami."
"For real, where at," she asked, I sent her the address of the hotel.
"That's 10 minutes from me," she replied to the location sent.
"What's your plans tonight? I want to see you."
"I'm studying for this exam. I'll let you know when I'm done."
"Okay."

When the texting ended, I closed my eyes then dozed off for nearly 15 minutes. I don't know if it was a dream or the engine of a loud vehicle roaring. When I woke up, I immediately downloaded the Uber App, put my info in, and then requested a ride to South Beach.

There are three places in the country where the fun finds you. New Orleans, Vegas, and Miami. I don't care if you're with a group of people or you're alone strolling the street in those places; you will be somewhere drunk with random people. As soon as I stepped foot on Ocean Drive I went into boss mode. You couldn't be on Ocean Drive without confidence. The energy on the street was electrifying. My chin was held high; my shoulders were relaxed and the stroll was slicker than olive oil. The streets were crowded with people as if there wasn't a pandemic. Groups of men and women, couples, people drinking, dancing in the middle of the street, players hollering at shorty's and women poised to be chosen.

The Sex Symbol sweatshirt brought a multitude of attention in my direction. In the middle of finding a restaurant on the strip for a pescatarian; five or six people stopped me to compliment the sweatshirt. Every woman that praised my shirt I simply exchanged numbers and never called neither one.

I was sold when I located a restaurant that has seafood and good hip-hop music. There were two sections of the restaurant. There was a front where people dinned and in the far back sat a bar. The dining section was overly saturated so I went to the back where two ladies were sitting next to an empty chair.

One of the lady's heads was resting on the bar. The woman I settled next to was sugar brown complexation with slanted chinky eyes in a red short dress, exposing her thighs. I sparked a conversation with the woman who seemed like she was in a good state of mind.

"She must've had too many drinks." Those six words established a discussion. She mentioned that she was from Philadelphia. She mentioned her name, age, occupation, college degrees and went on considering other topics. This woman was put together well. She surely had a head on her shoulders. When the bartender slid their food on the table. The smell of whatever was cooked triggered the drunk friend to turn away from the table.

She leaned over with sweat dripping from her face full of misery then vomited on the floor. In mid-conversation, the woman with the red dress hurried to escort her friend to the bathroom. In the time, the ladies were in the bathroom I witnessed the busboy bust his ass on the throw up as he passed by rushing towards the kitchen not seeing the splattered mess on the floor. While the man struggled to lift himself off the ground, the women swiftly came out of the bathroom then exited the building. Another employee that worked in the restaurant assisted his co-worker then mopped the floor as he complained the whole entire time cleaning

When the mess was cleaned, two new thick ladies came in seeking a seat to squat their butts on. The ladies who I recently sat beside left plates full of food that haven't been touched on the table. So, the women seeking open chairs weren't sure if the empty seats beside me were available.

"Y'all can sit here," I said waving the ladies over.

"Someone sitting here." The thick coffee brown woman stood about 5'6". Everything was long; eyelashes, hot pink nails, wig, and big hoop earrings. She was dressed in a neon pink skirt and a half crop top exposing the belly ring and the humongous titties. Both of the women were fancy hood rats, they reminded me of the movie B.A.P.S.

"No," then I explain the chain of events that happened earlier.

"Sex Symbol. So, are you a Sex Symbol?" Asked the cinnamon woman who had meat on her bones as well. Her smile was full of braces. Everything was long on her too. The nails, eyelashes were the only difference; she wore a purple wig. She almost had the exact clothing on as the coffee woman instead of neon pink the color she wore was neon green.

"Yes. This is my clothing brand for my book publishing company." I answered.

"So, you're a writer." The cinnamon woman asked.
"Yes, I am," I said with so much pride.
"What you write about? I love to read." She continued
"I write erotic novels, sexual fantasies, and some stories with my personal experience."

"So you're nasty, I'm guessing you know how to fuck." The coffee brown woman interrupted.

"I know some things," I answered.

"Hmm, You're cute too, what's your name." The coffee brown woman complimented me all in the same sentence of asking my name.

I glared right in coffee's eyes starring deep in her spirit.

"My name is Tink. What's your?"

"I'm Candy." The coffee woman answered.

"And yours," I gave cinnamon the same exact glare I gave Candy.

"It's Miracle." She said with lust screaming in her eyes.

"Nice to meet the both of ya'll," I said giving the same lustful energy towards both ladies.

"Can I ask you a question?" Candy asked.

"What's up?"

"Why are you looking at us like you want to fuck?" Candy asked being forward.

"Maybe because I want to." I choked this complete stranger as I spoke and bit my bottom lip. She leaned her face in towards me as if she enjoyed every bit of this grasp. When I let loose the lady bartender seemed turned on by the choking actions. Miracle's eyes widen and the guy with his girlfriend nodded his head.

"Don't do this to me in here. I will fuck the shit out of you." Candy said.

"We both will." Miracle slipped in her two cents. She stood to her feet, walked around Candy then stepped in front of me to rub my beard.

"Do you think you can handle us both?" She said in a low tone.

Right after Miracle spoke, Candy stood up. Both ladies cornered me against the bar.

"If I couldn't handle ya'll, don't you think I would be running."

"Pull your dick out." Candy demanded.
"If I pull out. What you fin' to do with it. Go and touch it it's hard." I hissed like a snake. Candy reached down, slid her hands against the bulge of my black shorts. Her eyes lit up like a winning machine at a casino.

"Oh, I'm fucking you tonight." She continued "Feel his dick Mir." Miracle reached then had the same reaction. Candy pulled out her phone.

"What you doing tonight. I want you to come over." When I gave Candy my number Miracle's facial expression went sour. Her energy shifted dramatically.

In the middle of talking to the ladies, I received a text from the woman chocolate crush on Instagram.

"Wyd (What you doing?) I'm done studying?" After I gave Candy my number, Miracle was set to leave and on top of that, they were frustrated with the bartenders for not bringing them their drinks fast enough.

"I'm going call you in the next 30 minutes to see where you're at? We're going somewhere else." Candy said then both of the ladies hugged me one by one.

To be real with my readers. Even if the women offered me to come over right at the moment. I would have not gone. One, myself alone in Miami with strangers talking about sex the first five minutes of meeting them. I'm all for spontaneous sex but this could've been a setup. Two, when I received the text from my chocolate crush that canceled all plans. I texted my chocolate crush while I followed the GPS to Collins Avenue. Soon as I got to the street the Uber driver called

.

"Where are you?" he said rudely with a Cuban accent.
"At 620 Collins Avenue, off 7th Street."

The driver was at the hotel Precious and I was staying at which was 20 minutes away. The Cuban man canceled the trip then I canceled to put in the address to attempt to get another car.

"What are doing love?" I asked.
"I was waiting for you to reply back. I'm getting sleepy."
"I'm trying to get an Uber back to the hotel."
"Where you at?" she asked.
"In front of the Vans Store on Collins Avenue."
"I can pick you up."
"That would be better." While we're on the phone this cute red-boned woman walked past storming up the sidewalk, heels clicking the pavement talking on the phone in the middle of a heated conversation. The only words that caught my attention.

"Fuck you N***a. Don't get mad if I fuck someone tonight in Miami." With the phone in hand, I did a double-take but decided to let that toxic woman be. I felt for whatever man that was on the other end of the line. I paid another eight-dollar cancelation fee to cancel the Uber then I sent my chocolate crush my location. I stood on the corner of Collins and 7th Ave while cop cars flashed red and blue lights lighting up the night as they cleared the street in time for the 12 o'clock pandemic curfew. Collins Street was blocked off so I met chocolate crush on 6th and Washington Avenue somewhere near a bank. Though I have randomly met people on social media before in malls, clubs, or in the grocery store. It still blows my mind that photos can turn into reality. How you can touch the actual human, smell, taste, and experience the real thing instead of a picture.

She took me to a ghetto section of Miami. She explained when she was in Jersey, online searching for places she did a virtual tour then fell in with the apartment not knowing the location was in the middle of the hood. When sitting in the living room she had boxes of panties, bras, and sex toys on the coffee table, next to a computer, and two phones with packaging supplies beside them. There were unpacked boxes against the walls and beside me was a lamp on a small table.

"I have to send these photos before I forget." She grasped one of the phones from the table then lifted her foot in the air; reaching for something on the floor.

"Wait, you sell foot flicks?" I asked.
"Yes. Can you oil my feet for me?" Chocolate rush toes were photogenic; her feet were a work of art with the glossy bright orange."
"People actually pay for feet pics," I asked, while she was texting the client with the foot fetish.

"Yes. You would be surprised." She said as I stroked her feet with oily hands. When the Cash App went through she showed me the $40 the man sent. He sent a photo of how he wanted the picture taken. She snapped the picture of her feet exactly cloning the photo sent.

In the short time, we both knew what we had a desire for, we both were in high demand for one other. We both were sex goats. She sold sex toys, lingerie, she a retired dancer, and wrote sexual blogs. Myself, a sex coach, an erotic author, and very experienced.

I felt guilty for being at this woman's house but in the same feeling, I knew the end result will be extravagant. I would not be here if the hotel door wouldn't have slammed as I stood outside on the balcony. I could've been the better man and straightened the issue by explaining what I had lined up for the birthday woman who brought me to the Sunshine State. There was no turning back now. We were both naked in the bedroom, the A/C blowing cool air in the middle of February. Chocolate crush's body was a natural with gold glitter spread all over, her ass soft with a nice hump with beautiful stretch marks, and her stomach flat with waist beads. Did I mention her body was dipped in pure chocolate?

"Lay down." She demanded. I reclined back on the mattress and put the nearest pillow under my head. Before I could get fully settled, my manhood was down the throat of my chocolate crush. The non-volume television shining gave the dark room light as Tank "When We" played on her phone. A buildup of saliva saturated all over my hardness, she whipped the length of this black dick against her hanging tongue, curled her hands around my thickness then created a splashing wet mess as she rotated her wrist and threw her neck; not giving a fuck about her throat.
"Ohh, you're nasty nasty," I said placing a hand over her short-cut hair. she was inhaling me in such a way I couldn't explain. She was sucking, slurping, blowing bubbles, and moaning. Her pride in sucking this love stick caused every single hair in my body to stand from the stimulating static. I felt her saliva streaming down my genitals, down between my ass cheeks then soaking into the sheets. In the middle of chocolate crush putting her face to work, I interrupted.
I had to distribute that same oral energy.

"Lay your ass down it's my turn." She surrendered her body to me, laid back, anticipating my next move. I attempted to plant soft kisses on her thighs, but by the way, she reacted, I knew she was ticklish. Instead of foreplay, I went straight for the source. I stuffed my face in between her thighs then allowed my tongue to perform its good deeds.

In the time my tongue whipped the clit I instantly felt her thighs tighten. Her moans grew as I identified her spot. I consistently aimed directly at that spot. Her entire body became solidified as I took her to a peak.
"Oh, shit oh shit! She let out curse words as she held my head in her pussy while I continued to lick her inner being. Chocolate crush scissored my face shut as she tried to crawl back away from my slitter.
"You have a condom."
"I don't." I had no clue that I was going to land in pussy.
"I have some." She stood up out of the bed, left the room for a hot five seconds then came in with a handful of condoms. She grasped one out the bunch, slid the rubber down the pipe, I laid back on the bed. She hovered over my stiffness then inched her way down without hurry.

"It's so big. It's so big." She reminded me on the way down. Chocolate crush wet box was seriously tight. I mean her walls were gripping like baseball batting gloves but wet like a water slide.

"It's so big," she bounced in a moderate rhythm.

People assume that women who are exotic dancers or women who display their bodies for money are hoes. When some of these ladies read books that half of these women wouldn't open if there were a million-dollar check inside. They'll show the world their bodies but be celibate or fucking less than a churchwoman that's not married.

I glanced down at her juices sliding as she went down and up me. Her hands planted on my chest moans seeped out her lips, her neck was loose cause her head to rock back and

forth. Time went on she swung her hips some more; riding the fuck out of me. I pulled her upper body towards mine the lifted my waist as she dropped down on me.
"Fuck. fuck. Fuck." She paused for a second. I kept on lifting my waist upward. In a countdown of 20 seconds, she was shaking insanely all while she climaxed on my throbbing black pole.

I came twice. We literally had amazing sex all through the night until 6am. It was still dark during this time of the year. I had to be back at the hotel before sunlight arrived. My chocolate crush gave me a ride back to the hotel. I got in the room slipped into the bed. Soon as I noticed the sun peeking through the window, I hurried to get in the shower to wash the gold glitter off my body. It was now Valentine's Day; I've got dressed went to Whole Foods then bought roses and chocolate strawberries. This all was a bitchassness move. I told her I'd got stuck in the lobby of a hotel because I could not get an Uber, my phone died. I felt terrible but not regretful.

The icing on the cake was when we came to my house from the airport, on my porch, there were several gifts on my porch for Valentine's Day. After this day, Precious blocked me on all social media, never called again. When she left, she tatted a quote in my mind.

"If you were more focused on reality other than women, you will be so far ahead."

She was right. I allowed myself to be clouded with the abundance of women my entire life. One Relationship to another relationship, old women to new women, one-night hook-ups to daily hook-ups, bar dates to dinner dates. Where do I have to grow? There's nowhere in this book where I explain how I became wealthy. In the past five months, I have starved myself from having the lavishness of women.

I've made double the amount of money I received monthly. I was able to write a book in four months with 50,000 words. Only if you knew how much alone time a person obligates to have to write a book. More blessings are to come.

I'm sorry for everyone I hurt.

The End

If you loved this book, don't forget to leave me a review on Amazon. Thanks for taking this journey with me.

Tinker Jeffries

www.sexsymbolstore.com
www.facebook.com/authortinkerjeffries
www.twitter.com/sexsymbol_tink
www.instagram.com/sexsymbol_tink
Sexsymboltink@gmail.com

Made in the USA
Middletown, DE
26 September 2023

39296556R00096